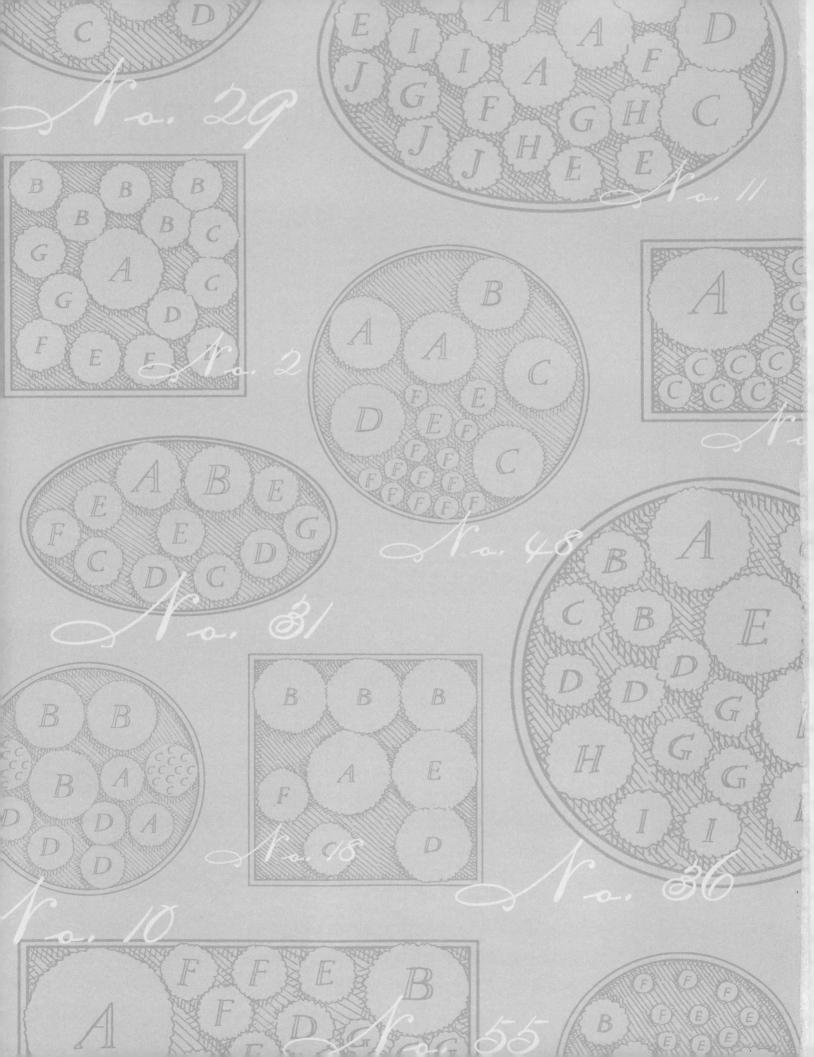

P. Allen Smith's

CONTAINER
GARDENS

P. Allen Smith's

CONTAINER GARDENS

60 Container Recipes to Accent Your Garden

PHOTOGRAPHS BY JANE COLCLASURE AND KELLY QUINN

DESIGN BY DINA DELL'ARCIPRETE/dk DESIGN PARTNERS INC, NYC

CLARKSON POTTER/PUBLISHERS
NEW YORK

Published by Clarkson Potter/Publishers, New York, New York
Member of the Crown Publishing Group,
a division of Random House, Inc.
www.clarksonpotter.com

CLARKSON N. POTTER is a trademark and POTTER and
colophon are registered trademarks of Random House, Inc.

Printed in Japan

Garden plan illustrations by Ken Krug

Library of Congress Cataloging-in-Publication Data
Smith, P. Allen.
P. Allen Smith's container gardens: 60 container recipes to accent
your garden / P. Allen Smith; photographs by Jane Colclasure
and Kelly Quinn. 1. Container gardening. 2. Recipes.
I. Title: Container gardens.   II. Title.
SB418.S64 2005
635.9'86—dc22   2004016327

ISBN 1-4000-5343-9

10 9 8 7 6 5 4 3 2 1

First Edition

Small green glazed bottles encircle a container of burro's tail (Sedum morganianum).

To Kee Kee

Planted containers came to my rescue when I was faced with a challenging design project at an early point in my career. To help raise funds for the local symphony, a stately old home in the historic district was to undergo a complete makeover inside and out. Selected designers were invited to showcase their talents by remodeling the house and grounds, and upon completion the public was invited to tour the results.

While I was excited to be one of the garden designers invited to participate, I could see that there were three major challenges that needed to be addressed immediately—there was no budget, detailed plans were needed right away, and the opening was slated for early spring. The first two problems didn't seem nearly as daunting as the last. The real dilemma was that the open house was scheduled so early in the season that I knew it would be difficult to find fully flowered, mature plants. As a designer, I am used to creating "instant gardens" for garden shows and special occasions by employing some tricks of the trade to give an area an established look, but the timing of this event would require more than smoke and mirrors to pull off a memorable design.

OPPOSITE, ABOVE LEFT: *Sedum spills over the lip of a cast-iron container atop a pedestal.* ABOVE RIGHT: *The color volume of a mixed border is bumped up a notch by dropping in a container of hot pink geraniums.* LOWER LEFT: *A cottage-style border is created by clustering several containers together.* LOWER RIGHT: *English boxwoods in simple terra-cotta containers soften the line between house and garden.*

I was on a mission. A quick, intensive search for plants yielded some colorful but low-growing bedding material, but I could find only a few perennials tall enough to give the area substantial mass or height. I panicked. My options appeared limited, tickets were selling like hotcakes, and the deadline was looming. That's when I seized upon the idea of using containers.

My assigned area was a prominent flower border that was lined on one side by a walkway and on the other side by a long, low stone wall backed with a boxwood hedge. I wanted to give the border some movement, so I planted a thick sinuous line of bright pink begonias running the entire length of the bed. Next, I added splashes of pink and purple violas, pansies, and pincushion flowers in the foreground. Behind the line of begonias, I popped in some spring flowering bulbs, planting the pots and all, so they appeared as though the blooms had just emerged. Amid these festive colors I sprinkled in several other varieties of early-spring flowers.

As the main attraction, I stuffed three large terra-cotta containers with all the Louisiana irises I could find and rhythmically placed them throughout the bed. That was it! The size and scale of the containers filled with the tall lance-shaped foliage of the iris added just the right touch of drama and height.

I was pleased with the results and enjoyed the reactions from touring guests. That success encouraged me to experiment with other ways to incorporate containers in landscape plans. I soon discovered that they were a beautiful solution for many of my design dilemmas simply because of their flexibility.

Since containers can be positioned wherever flowers or foliage are needed, even in areas where there is no soil, I use them frequently. Much like interior accessories, they are easily rearranged to create colorful accents and eye-catching focal points, or to change the mood or style of an outdoor area.

In my first book, *P. Allen Smith's Garden Home*, I shared key principles of design to help homeowners expand the beauty and comfort of their homes into their gardens. Containers played an important role in creating the look and style of those areas. I used them to frame the view beneath a window, offer a welcoming reception to an entrance, establish a sense of rhythm along a walkway, and extend a home's color and décor into the garden.

To inspire you to take full advantage of the many ways to use containers in your garden home, this book offers sixty of my best "recipes" presented as a container cookbook. Not only will you find complete lists of ingredients to help you duplicate the designs, but I also offer ideas for placement of the containers to enhance your garden's beauty and style.

As you thumb through the seasonal selections of sun and shade containers, you are sure to find several designs to complement your home's character. Some planting designs may be exact models of what you want to create, while others may serve as springboards to fashion your own personal statement. Just as in cooking, the recipes are there as a formula for success and also as a framework to encourage you to add your own special twist.

In recognizing that these containers will be used all over the country, the container recipes rely heavily on plants that grow in a wide range of hardiness zones. The plant directory in the back of the book will provide you with additional information on each plant. There, you'll also find lists of the essential items I use in my potting shed, ideas for creating an area for potting your plants, and some key planting techniques and maintenance practices.

I hope this book will encourage you to explore the world of container gardens and discover the many ways in which they can enhance the beauty of your garden home. Even if you have never turned a shovel of earth, you can enjoy a glorious garden brimming with color and style. You will soon discover that container plants can be used everywhere: on your front step, in a flowerbed, by your mailbox, under a tree, on a deck or patio, hanging from an eave, and under your windows. That's the real beauty of these portable gardens; there is always room for one more.

OPPOSITE, ABOVE LEFT: *A bird's-eye view of the garden designed for the Symphony House fundraiser illustrates how large containers can add volume and drama to a newly planted flower border.* ABOVE RIGHT: *'New Dawn' rose scampers up a rustic trellis amid 'Cascadia Improved Charlie' purple petunias, 'Blueberry Sachet' nemesia, 'Rapunzel Pink' verbena, 'Penny Blue' violas, and 'Helene Von Stein' lamb's ear.* BELOW LEFT: *The gorgeous blue flower clusters of lily of the Nile (agapanthus) add a tropical feel to the patio.* BELOW RIGHT: Containers of pink pincushion flowers (scabiosa), geraniums, and 'Penny Blue' violas create a flower-strewn entry up the steps to the porch.

The creation of something new is not accomplished by the intellect but by the play of instinct acting from inner necessity. The creative mind plays with the objects it loves.

—CARL JUNG

Planting containers is the perfect way to play in the garden. With an armload of plants, a bag of soil, and the container of your choice, you can put together a gorgeous bouquet of blooms to enhance the beauty of your home. It's a low-risk method of experimenting with all kinds of plants to discover new and exciting combinations. And best of all, it's an activity you can enjoy year round. Every season brings a new palette of colors to enliven your garden.

Containers have become an indispensable part of my garden designs. By merely altering the sizes and styles of containers and the varieties of plants, these portable gardens can be fashioned into privacy screens, focal points, entry accents, and tabletop centerpieces. The number of ways they can be transformed to strengthen a garden's design is limited only by the imagination.

Each recipe in this book is designated to meet one of my 12 Principles of Design, as described in my first book, *P. Allen Smith's Garden Home*, and summarized on page 179. A principle is listed with every recipe as a guide to help you place containers to their best advantage in your garden.

OPPOSITE: *Spiky grasses wave in the breeze, welcoming guests entering the garden. The bright blue container filled with blue ageratum, Cuban oregano, blue agastache, and silver sedge enlivens the pathway through the gate.*

Because they are so useful, I find myself constantly designing, planting, and rearranging containers. This experience has helped me discover some effective methods of assembling planters that you may find helpful.

My first suggestion is to approach the design of a container as if it were a flower arrangement using a method I call the Three-Shape Rule. The idea is to combine three basic plant forms in each arrangement. For many people, this requires looking at plants in a new way. Instead of focusing on a plant's colorful flowers or foliage, look at its overall outline or silhouette. When you do this, you'll discover that most plants fall into one of three general forms: tall and spiky, round and full, or trailing and cascading. Whenever I arrange a combination of plants from each of these categories, it results in a more appealing and dynamic design. These three basic forms complement one another so well that it doesn't really matter if the plants ever bloom. This method allows you to use plants that have great-looking foliage as well as those with colorful flowers. As you look through the book, you'll find that many of my designs are variations on this theme.

Another method I use to design containers is to choose mature plants. This is just the opposite of what I usually do when I'm planting a flower border. There, I select immature plants that haven't yet flowered so that their initial energy is directed into putting down roots, not pushing out blooms. But when it comes to containers, I'm looking for instant impact. So when I go to a garden center, I select big plants, preferably with lots of blooms and buds that are in gallon- or quart-sized containers, or even in hanging basket size.

Often the containers I design are meant to look complete as soon as they are planted because I like to display them right away. If I'm hosting a party or special event, I'll assemble several containers to enliven the festivities. Sometime later I may decide to remove some of the plants and reuse them either in another design or in my flowerbeds. I find that potted plants behave much like those in my planted borders in that they tend to ebb and flow in their performance. Because a potted arrangement is a concentration of plants, if one begins to fade, it tends to diminish the appeal of the entire composition, so I'll pull it out and replace it with something in its prime to keep the container looking its best.

You may prefer to plant a container and enjoy it throughout the growing season. Many of the recipes are designed to be especially well suited for that purpose. You will discover that as the weeks go by, the arrangement will evolve as the plants settle in and continue to grow. At that time you can decide to either prune back some of the more exuberant participants in your ensemble or allow them to take center stage. I consider this all part of the editing process. Unlike a flower arrangement, container plants continue to grow, each at their own rate, giving the composition a dynamic quality that I enjoy.

I also find it entertaining to change the look of my arrangements by rotating plants in and out of containers. Few plants go to waste as I repurpose nearly every one, unless it isn't healthy. Some are combined with other plants to create new container arrangements, others are transplanted into my flower borders, and still others are repotted into smaller containers and wait in the wings near my potting shed until they are needed again. If you haven't considered this approach, I suggest you try it. There is no better way to build your confidence in mixing plants and trying new color combinations than to plant several containers throughout the year and remodel them as you see fit.

Container gardening is truly an activity that you can enjoy year round. There is no better way to add bursts of color and life to your garden home than with gorgeous planted containers. And remember, the combinations you find successful on a small scale can be expanded to your flower borders.

FOLLOWING THE RECIPES

As you prepare your shopping list and head to the garden center, keep in mind that all plants are not created (or grow) equal. Although my recipes list plants according to their container size (quart or gallon), you will find that there really isn't anything standard about the size of typical nursery pots. And as you may have noticed, plants grow at different rates in their nursery pots. Occasionally, I have found larger plants in a quart container than those in a gallon-sized pot.

As I look for plants at a nursery, I usually don't focus on the container, but instead I look at the size of the plant and put it next to other plants I'm using in the arrangement to see how they combine. I do this by gathering all the plants that I need in a cart and then taking them to an area of the nursery where I can lay them out and see how they look together. If a plant appears out of proportion to the others, I go back and find a better size, or in some cases, select two plants that I can combine to get the size or fullness I need.

Because I'm a bargain shopper, I often hunt for a two gallon–sized plant growing in a one-gallon container. The motto I follow is: look at the plant first and then the size of the pot. Going for a larger plant in a smaller pot than is recommended in the recipe is fine; just be sure it is vigorous, disease-free, and not root-bound. If most of a plant's roots are growing out of the drainage holes or if they form a tight circle at the bottom of the pot, that's not a good sign. Both are indications that the plant has outgrown its container, and may not be healthy.

In fact, giving every plant you buy, no matter its size, a quick checkup to make sure it is vigorous is a good idea. For more ideas on how to select healthy nursery plants, read my tips on page 188.

I encourage you to study the photographs of the finished containers and take note of how the plants compare in size in

relation to one another. It may be helpful to take this book along to the garden center as a reminder.

In that same spirit, if you can't find the variety of plant listed in the recipe, study its characteristics and find one that has a similar shape, form, and color with comparable growth habits. For example, if a dwarf Alberta spruce is listed and it isn't available in your area or is not well suited for your climate, find another evergreen with similar characteristics as a substitute. Just be sure the stand-in is suited to grow in the same light and water conditions. Qualified garden center staff should be able to help you find good substitutions.

The most important thing is to enjoy the process. What I love most about container gardening is the sense of satisfaction from completing a project in just a few minutes. In no time at all I can create a decorative accent that will provide months of enjoyment. I hope you'll find that once you get started, you, too, will be immersed in the pleasure of mixing up batches of your own container recipes.

SPRiNG

I know that spring has finally arrived when my first conscious thought as I awaken in the morning is the list of things that I want to accomplish in the garden. I can't bear to miss a single moment as my plants emerge from their winter slumber. I want to witness every leaf unfolding and breathe in the sweet fragrance of each new flower. If only there was a way to cast a wide net and capture all the abundance of the season.

DURING THOSE FIRST WARM, SPRING DAYS, EVERYTHING IN THE GARDEN SEEMS TO NEED ATTENTION AT ONCE. THERE IS SO MUCH TO DO, I CAN'T HELP BUT FEEL A BIT FRANTIC. I AM EAGER TO FILL MY GARDEN WITH NEW PLANTS, BUT I KNOW ALL TOO WELL THAT THE WEATHER IS FAR FROM SETTLED AND TEMPERATURES CAN BOUNCE UP AND DOWN LIKE BRANCHES IN A MARCH WIND.

That's when I turn to container gardens as a safe outlet for my need to plant. I'm free to fill pots and planters full of early-spring blooms knowing I can easily cover or move the containers indoors should freezing temperatures make an unwelcome visit.

My first pots are often filled with the gentle colors of the season: pastel pinks and soft purples, along with bright yellow and my favorite spring color, blue. There are so many beautiful early blue flowers that I can't help but go a little crazy planting as many as I can find: grape hyacinths, 'Penny Azure Twilight' violas, blue pansies, even tiny blue iris reticulata. There don't seem to be enough containers to hold all of the possibilities.

This is also the time when I pull out the pots that I've kept on hold in my lathe house. It feels as if I have discovered hidden treasure when I haul out container after container of spring-flowering bulbs that I planted last fall and tucked away under my potting bench. Yellow and white daffodils along with lively shades of salmon and deep pink tulips have emerged and are ready to be added to new containers or clustered together with other planted pots. Despite years of experience in the garden, this rite of spring continues to be pure magic to me.

Consider planting shrubs, trees, and vines in containers as eye-catching accents in your garden. A pair of wisteria vines supported by bamboo poles creates a simple and elegant welcome to this garden entrance.

things to keep in mind

* ✳ Remove both the tulips and the hyacinths after the blooms fade, and allow the artemisia and lettuce to fill in.
* ✳ Look for other opportunities to mix lettuce into spring flowering containers.

PARTIAL SUN • Garden Home Principle: **COLOR**

I. Bold Lettuce and Spring Bulbs

This lively duo makes a great accent for the steps leading up to a back door. The color of the 'Red Sail' lettuce leaves is great with the terra-cotta containers and adds depth to the pink shades of the flowering spring bulbs.

2   round terra-cotta pots
- Large—16 inches diameter × 14 inches deep
- Small—12 inches diameter × 11 inches deep

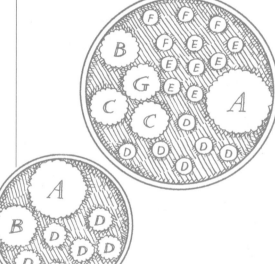

LARGE CONTAINER

1   1-gallon 'Evergold' sedge (*Carex hachijoensis* 'Evergold')
1   1-quart strawberry foxglove (*Digitalis × mertonensis*)
2   1-quart 'Peach Sachet' nemesia (*Nemesia × hybrida* 'Peach Sachet')
1   6-pack 'Red Sail' lettuce (*Lactuca sativa* 'Red Sail')
5   bulbs 'Top Hit' pink hyacinths (*Hyacinthus orientalis* "Top Hit')
6–8 bulbs 'Gorden Cooper' pink tulips (*Tulipa* 'Gorden Cooper')
1   1-quart 'Oriental Limelight' artemisia (*Artemisia vulgaris* 'Oriental Limelight')

SMALL CONTAINER

1   1-gallon 'Evergold' sedge (*Carex hachijoensis* 'Evergold')
1   1-quart strawberry foxglove (*Digitalis × mertonensis*)
1   6-pack 'Red Sail' lettuce (*Lactuca sativa* 'Red Sail')

The first time I saw 'Red Sail' lettuce growing in a group of pots in a kitchen garden in England, it looked so luxurious I thought, What a great idea, why not use it in a container? Since then, I have mixed this loose-leaf lettuce into many planters with great success.

This design incorporates lettuce, along with foxglove, spring bulbs, and nemesia. When not in bloom, the foxglove works well as a dark green foliage accent. The intense chartreuse of the artemisia brings to life the monochromatic color combination, and the grasslike foliage of the sedge serves as a nice textural foil. When combining two pots such as these, a variation in height creates more visual appeal.

This plant combination maintains its charm throughout the cool days of spring and is a good opportunity to experiment with other cool-season varieties of lettuce and vegetables like broccoli, Swiss chard, and spinach. All these leafy vegetables add a nice touch of texture and an unexpected twist to otherwise traditional flowering containers.

Plant List

A. 'Evergold' sedge
B. Strawberry foxglove
C. 'Peach Sachet' nemesia
D. 'Red Sail' lettuce
E. 'Top Hit' pink hyacinths
F. 'Gorden Cooper' pink tulips
G. 'Oriental Limelight' artemisia

PARTIAL SUN • Garden Home Principle: **COLOR**

2. Vivid Blue Contemporary Design

Bright-colored glazed containers bring a sparkle to the garden, but it can be challenging to find the right plants to work with their scene-stealing color. When coupled with a variety of richly hued flowers and foliage, the bright blue color of this square ceramic planter makes a wonderful poolside accent.

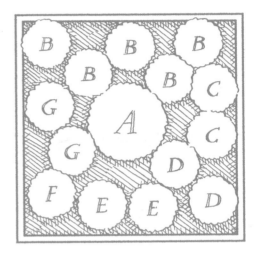

1 blue square glazed ceramic container—
  16 inches tall × 16 inches diameter × 15 inches deep
1 1-gallon bell flower hesperaloë (*Hesperaloë campanulata*)
5 1-quart 'Brightside' Sunscape daisy (*Osteospermum fruticosum* 'Brightside')
2 1-quart 'Glacier' English ivy (*Hedera helix* 'Glacier')
2 1-quart purple heart (*Tradescantia pallida*)
2 1-quart 'Blue Showers' bacopa (*Sutera cordata* 'Blue Showers')
1 1-quart 'Bronze Beauty' ajuga (*Ajuga reptans* 'Bronze Beauty')
2 1-quart silver sedge (*Carex platyphylla*)

Eye-popping color always grabs my attention. When I came across a sea of 'Brightside' osteospermum flowers at a local nursery, I couldn't help but notice that the center eye of the flower was a close match to this bright blue container. It's just astonishing what nature (with the help of plant breeders) can come up with! So, with 'Brightside' as the centerpiece for this design, I looked for the right plants to combine with it.

Plants that have movement and depth are important here because they offset the angular shape of the container. The bell flower hesperaloë, with its tall, gracefully arching foliage, gives the arrangement a dynamic quality. The purple heart's, or wandering Jew's, deep purple foliage helps to ground the arrangement and offset the bright blue container while also helping to give the arrangement some depth. The bacopa and ivy finish off the composition by spilling over the edge and softening the strong lines of the planter.

Plant List
A. *Bell flower hesperaloë*
B. *'Brightside' Sunscape daisy*
C. *'Glacier' English ivy*
D. *Purple heart*
E. *'Blue Showers' bacopa*
F. *'Bronze Beauty' ajuga*
G. *Silver sedge*

things to keep in mind
❋ As temperatures rise, the plants will do better with some afternoon shade.
❋ Select a plant that echoes the color of the container, then add complementary plants to build the arrangement.

'BRIGHTSIDE' SUNSCAPE DAISY

BELL FLOWER HESPERALOË

'GLACIER' ENGLISH IVY

SILVER SEDGE

PURPLE HEART

'BRONZE BEAUTY' AJUGA

'BLUE SHOWERS' BACOPA

· No. 2 ·

SUN • Garden Home Principle: **WHIMSY**

3. Bountiful Spring Baskets

As spring awakens and shakes off its winter coat, the freshness of a new season enlivens the spirit in us all. Capture that moment with these happy baskets of blooms.

2   wire baskets
- Large basket—12 inches diameter × 11 inches deep
- Small basket—10 inches diameter × 9 inches deep

2   large packages of sphagnum moss
2   dark-colored garbage sacks

LARGE BASKET

3   1-quart 'Vanilla Sachet' nemesia (*Nemesia × hybrida* 'Vanilla Sachet')
3   1-quart 'Penny Azure Twilight' viola (*Viola cornuta* 'Penny Azure Twilight')
5   bulbs blue hyacinth (*Hyacinthus orientalis*)

SMALL BASKET

2   1-quart 'Vanilla Sachet' nemesia (*Nemesia × hybrida* 'Vanilla Sachet')
2   1-quart 'Penny Azure Twilight' viola (*Viola cornuta* 'Penny Azure Twilight')
2   5-inch pots (20 to 24 bulbs total) 'Valerie Finnis' muscari (*Muscari armeniacum* 'Valerie Finnis')

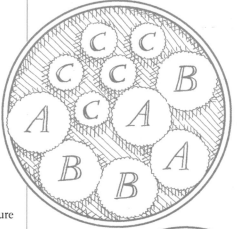

Spring can arrive in a flash and leave just as suddenly. This arrangement helps capture the season's brief, ephemeral beauty in soft shades of blue and purple. The baskets are filled with sweet scented muscari and the delightful blooms of nemesia and viola.

The open-wire baskets are lined with sphagnum moss that is presoaked to make it easier to mold to the shape of the basket. (A plastic garbage bag serves as a liner inside each basket. Be sure to poke holes in the plastic so that the water can drain properly.) Fill the lined baskets with potting mix and then pack them with blooms. These delightfully simple displays are easily moved from one location to another.

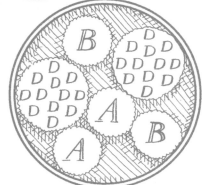

things to keep in mind

* Be sure to keep the arrangements well watered. Because of the baskets' open-wire weave, the plants can dry out quickly.
* Depending on where you place the baskets, you may want to put saucers under them so that water doesn't stain the area underneath.
* If kept in a cool, shaded area, the blooms last for a long time. The nemesia and violas fill in after the muscari are finished blooming.

Plant List

A. *'Vanilla Sachet' nemesia*
B. *'Penny Azure Twilight' viola*
C. *Blue hyacinth*
D. *'Valerie Finnis' muscari*

SUN • Garden Home Principle: **SHAPE AND FORM**

4. Colorful Herb-Filled Trough

For the treasure hunter in all of us, part of the fun of container gardening is searching for out-of-the-ordinary planters. This turquoise concrete trough was a yard sale find. The plant forms in the arrangement and the bright container are best appreciated when displayed at eye level in the center of a deck or patio table.

I	Turquoise (or other color of choice) concrete trough— 24 inches long × 8 inches wide × 10 inches deep
I	1-gallon 'Salem' rosemary (*Rosmarinus officinalis* 'Salem')
I	1-gallon chives (*Allium schoenoprasum*)
I	1-quart lamb's ear (*Stachys byzantina*)
2	1-quart 'Butterfly Blue' scabiosa (*Scabiosa columbaria* 'Butterfly Blue')
3	3-inch pots fern-leaf lavender (*Lavandula pinnata*)
I	6-pack purple cabbage (*Brassica oleracea*)
2	6-packs 'Penny Azure Twilight' viola (*Viola cornuta* 'Penny Azure Twilight')

Plant List

A. *'Salem' rosemary*

B. *Chives*

C. *Lamb's ear*

D. *'Butterfly Blue' scabiosa*

E. *Fern-leaf lavender*

F. *Purple cabbage*

G. *'Penny Azure Twilight' viola*

Even when it comes to garden containers, colors seem to come and go. I am willing to bet that this turquoise trough was all the rage in the 1950s and 1960s, until the color became passé and fell out of favor. Now, decades later, it works again. Container gardening is a great opportunity to take a container color that is somewhat challenging and find the right plants to showcase it.

The combined shades of gray, purple, and lavender work quite well in this arrangement. The broad leaves of the cabbage play off the fine foliage of the rosemary and chives, enlivening the composition with some contrasting textures. The purple cabbage also adds some dimension to the arrangement with its darker color. For a bit of sparkle, the blooms of the 'Penny' violas and a pincushion flower finish off the look.

The container is filled with lots of edible plants: violas, chives, rosemary, and cabbage—making it not only beautiful but useful as well. Early spring offers a great opportunity to use broad-leafed vegetable plants like cabbage and broccoli in container plantings, because they can handle severe drops in temperatures.

things to keep in mind

* Make sure that no pesticides have been used on any of the edible plants you harvest from the containers.

* As the summer progresses, the cool-season cabbage and violas can be replaced with purple verbena, red oxalis, and 'Trailing Plum' coleus and the arrangement can be lightened with the silvery gray foliage of dusty miller.

PURPLE CABBAGE

CHIVES

'SALEM' ROSEMARY

FERN-LEAF LAVENDER

'PENNY AZURE TWILIGHT' VIOLA

'BUTTERFLY BLUE' SCABIOSA

LAMB'S EAR

• No. 4 •

things to keep in mind
* The Japanese andromeda shrubs can reside happily in the container, or be transplanted into the landscape.
* If you move the hellebores into your garden (Zones 4–9), site them in a dappled-shade location where the soil is rich in humus. Once established, they will perform for years, requiring little care.

PARTIAL SHADE • Garden Home Principle: **ABUNDANCE**

5. Dramatic Early-Spring Container

The transition from one season to the next opens the door to a fresh variety of exciting plant combinations. Load up containers with an abundance of plants to give them that bursting-with-spring feeling. Place this arrangement close to a frequently used pathway or near steps leading up to your front door.

1 Terra-cotta container—24 inches diameter × 17 inches deep
2 1-gallon 'Valley Rose' Japanese andromeda (*Pieris japonica* 'Valley Rose')
5 1-gallon 'Royal Heritage' strain hellebore (*Helleborus* 'Royal Heritage')
2 1-gallon English ivy (*Hedera helix*)
2 1-gallon Chinese wild ginger (*Asarum splendens*)

Offering a hint of the emerging season while making use of late-winter finds is the theme of this plant combination. I found these hellebores and Japanese andromeda shrubs loaded with buds and on sale in the garden center in the dead of winter. Although the andromeda were not perfectly formed (and probably left over from the previous season) I wedded two of them together by matching their weaker sides to create what appeared to be one full plant. Keep in mind that shrubs such as these do best in large containers because there is more room for the roots and the soil won't dry out as quickly.

All of these plants are shade lovers and are at their best during those cool days of early spring. The container can take center stage while the plants are in their peak and then it can be moved to a quiet corner of the garden once the show is over.

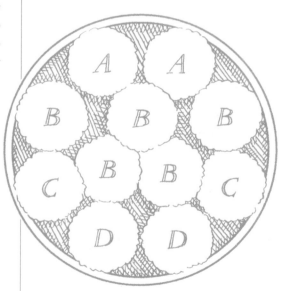

Plant List
A. *'Valley Rose' Japanese andromeda*
B. *'Royal Heritage' strain hellebore*
C. *English ivy*
D. *Chinese wild ginger*

PARTIAL SHADE • Garden Home Principle: **WHIMSY**

6. Classic Urn for Shade

Mixing a loose, carefree combination of plants with a stately cast-iron urn unites opposites in an appealing way. A pair of these containers on either side of a formal iron gate offers a friendly and sophisticated welcome to guests.

1   Black-green cast-iron urn—18 inches diameter × 17 inches tall
     (with 13-inch inside diameter)
1   1-gallon 'Snowcap' hosta (*Hosta* 'Snow Cap')
2   1-quart 'Golden Baby' ivy (*Hedera helix* 'Golden Baby')
2   1-quart 'Bronze Beauty' ajuga (*Ajuga reptans* 'Bronze Beauty')
1   1-quart sea-pinks (*Armeria maritima* 'Splendens')

Many times when I select plants to use in a container, I'm never quite sure how the arrangement will look until it is planted. I often feel my way through a design and find I am as surprised as anyone with the results. When I finished this one, I couldn't quite put my finger on why I found it so appealing. Then it struck me: the whole arrangement has the feel of one of those outrageous classic hats that you see at Easter. What fun!

The ornate black urn stands in formal contrast to the effervescent colors of the plants. 'Golden Baby' ivy bubbles over the rim, spilling out seemingly everywhere. The blue spikes of ajuga nestled up against the sea-pinks and the jaunty angle of the 'Snowcap' hosta seem to give a wink to the stately presence of the urn.

things to keep in mind

* A playful composition in a grand container can create just the right balance.
* Heavy containers are best positioned first and then planted.

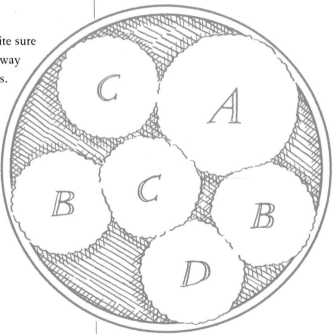

Plant List
A. *'Snowcap' hosta*
B. *'Golden Baby' ivy*
C. *'Bronze Beauty' ajuga*
D. *Sea-pinks*

'SNOWCAP' HOSTA

'GOLDEN BABY' IVY

'BRONZE BEAUTY' AJUGA

SEA-PINKS

· No. 6 ·

abundance

'BLUE SHADES' COLUMBINE

'SUM AND SUBSTANCE' HOSTA

BLUE HYACINTH

LADY FERN

GOLDEN CREEPING JENNY

'SWEET KATE' SPIDERWORT

· No. 7 ·

SHADE • Garden Home Principle: **TEXTURE, PATTERN, AND RHYTHM**

7. Chartreuse and Blue Shade Garden

Lacy, broad, and refined are traits that have been woven together in this tapestry of shade-loving plants. Place the container next to a hammock, a quiet reading spot, or a meditation bench as a calming influence.

1 round black metal container—19 inches diameter × 16 inches deep
1 1-gallon 'Sum and Substance' hosta (*Hosta* 'Sum and Substance')
2 1-gallon 'Blue Shades' columbine (*Aquilegia* hybrids 'Blue Shades')
3 1-gallon lady fern (*Athyrium filix-femina*)
2 1-quart 'Sweet Kate' spiderwort (*Tradescantia × andersoniana* 'Sweet Kate')
3 1-quart golden creeping Jenny (*Lysimachia nummularia* 'Aurea')
3 bulbs blue hyacinth (*Hyacinthus orientalis*)

After seeing a massive 'Sum and Substance' hosta growing in a container at the entrance to a home in Holland, I always wanted to use the plant in a similar way. What a picture it made with its bold leaves and electric color! A familiar combination of shade plants in this arrangement—lacy ferns, creeping Jenny, and a delicate columbine—play off the texture of the hosta's thick leathery leaves. These contrasting textures help to highlight each plant because of their striking differences from one another.

 Bright chartreuse foliage played against a dark gray or lead-colored container is a pleasing combination. The visual heaviness of the dark planter helps anchor the vibrant yellows and greens. This arrangement's chartreuse foliage combines with the blue and purple blooms of the hyacinth, columbine, and spiderwort to create a serene composition.

Plant List
A. *'Sum and Substance' hosta*
B. *'Blue Shades' columbine*
C. *Lady fern*
D. *'Sweet Kate' spiderwort*
E. *Golden creeping Jenny*
F. *Blue hyacinth*

things to keep in mind

✳ Once the hyacinths finish blooming, they should be pulled from the container.
✳ By early summer, the spring show of the columbine's blue blooms fades, but the lush green display will continue to glow even in the shade.

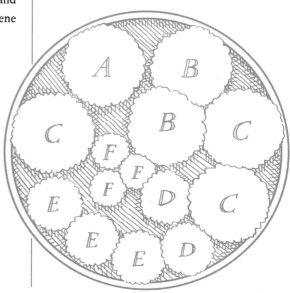

SUN • Garden Home Principle: **TEXTURE, PATTERN, AND RHYTHM**

8. Tulip-Filled Planter Box

This trio of dark green dwarf spruce creates a rhythmic backdrop for an array of colorful spring flowers. As the seasonal blooms fade, new plants can be added to create a continuous sequence of color. This planter box is sensational placed against a bare wall decorated with a single eye-catching architectural feature, such as a mask, hanging above it.

1   faux-lead/resin trough—33 inches long × 17 inches wide × 14 inches deep
3   1-gallon dwarf Alberta spruce (*Picea glauca* 'Conica')
4   1-quart golden creeping Jenny (*Lysimachia nummularia* 'Aurea')
4   1-quart 'Bronze Beauty' ajuga (*Ajuga reptans* 'Bronze Beauty')
2-3 6 packs 'Penny Blue' viola (*Viola cornuta* 'Penny Blue')
14-18 bulbs Triumph type, soft pink tulips—12 to 14 inches tall (*Tulipa* hybrids)

Tulips are real knockouts in this planter box, emerging from a sea of violas. Be generous when filling in the center of the planter, setting the bulbs "shoulder to shoulder." Creeping Jenny and ajuga join in the cozy display and spill over the sides of the container, softening the planter's edge.

   This arrangement sustains its beauty beyond the spring season. After the tulips fade, replace them with a series of pink dianthus or salmon geraniums. The ajuga and creeping Jenny stay on to become more lush and full as the season unfolds.

Plant List
A. *Dwarf Alberta spruce*
B. *Golden creeping Jenny*
C. *'Bronze Beauty' Ajuga*
D. *'Penny Blue' Viola*
E. *Triumph type tulips*

things to keep in mind

🟊 Invent your own similar recipe if these plant varieties aren't available in your area.

🟊 Alberta spruce can be substituted with another dwarf conical evergreen, creeping Jenny could be replaced with a golden variegated ivy, and if tulips aren't available, try other spring-flowering bulbs such as daffodils or hyacinths. Even the violas can be substituted with pansies or purple nemesia.

🟊 Make sure the stand-ins require the same water and light conditions.

BELL FLOWER HESPERALOË

'FROSTY MORN' SEDUM

'BRIGHTSIDE' SUNSCAPE DAISY

FERN LEAF LAVENDER

'GLACIER' ENGLISH IVY

'WHITE SACHET' NEMESIA

· No. 9 ·

PARTIAL SUN • Garden Home Principle: **FOCAL POINT**

9. Carefree Cape Daisy Combo

The advantage of this container is how well it blends with the other elements in the garden. Its quietly sophisticated color palette fits comfortably into almost any garden setting. Make the container a focal point by pairing the cast stone pot with a birdbath or piece of garden statuary.

1	cast-stone planter—19 inches diameter × 18 inches deep
2	1-gallon bell flower hesperaloë (*Hesperaloë campanulata*)
2	1-gallon 'Frosty Morn' sedum (*Sedum erythrostictum* 'Frosty Morn')
2	3-inch 'Glacier' English ivy (*Hedera helix* 'Glacier')
3	1-quart 'Brightside' Sunscape daisy (*Osteospermum* 'Brightside')
3	1-quart 'White Sachet' nemesia (*Nemesia × hybrida* 'White Sachet')
4	3-inch pots fern-leaf lavender (*Lavandula pinnata*)

I find the combination of frosty white plants in this weathered stone container to be just the right blend of relaxed elegance. The white petals of the blue-eyed 'Brightside' Sunscape daisies offer an especially fresh, lighthearted quality. The white and blue colors of the blooms are echoed throughout the composition, from the blue flowers of the fern leaf lavender floating above the pot to the silvery blue foliage of the bell flower. Shades of cream are mirrored in the leaf margins of the variegated ivy, the blossoms of the white nemesia, and in the grayed foliage of 'Frosty Morn' sedum.

Plant List

A. *Bell flower hesperaloë*
B. *'Frosty Morn' sedum*
C. *'Glacier' English ivy*
D. *'Brightside' Sunscape daisy*
E. *'White Sachet' nemesia*
F. *Fern-leaf lavender*

things to keep in mind

✳ This arrangement is best suited for the cooler temperatures of spring. The plants may languish in the heat of summer, but they will perk up in fall.

✳ As a fringe benefit, the pink flower heads of the sedum also emerge later in the season.

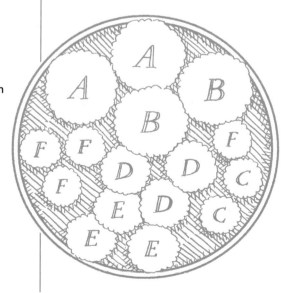

SUN • Garden Home Principle: **TEXTURE, PATTERN, AND RHYTHM**

10. Drought-Tolerant Sun Container

This design is an especially handsome choice for homes of a contemporary style. Rather than a sleek and highly stylized arrangement, the stone trough suggests a more casual statement. Many modern homes embrace a natural landscape, making this container a comfortable fit.

1	stone trough—19 inches diameter × 7 inches deep
2	1-quart 'Helene Von Stein' lamb's ear (*Stachys byzantina* 'Helene Von Stein')
3	1-gallon 'Bewitched' dianthus (*Dianthus gratianopolitanus* 'Bewitched')
2	5-inch pots (24 bulbs) 'Valerie Finnis' muscari (*Muscari armeniacum* 'Valerie Finnis')
4	1-quart hen and chicks (*Sempervivum* hybrids)

I jumped at the chance to use this stone container when a friend offered it to me. I had been on the hunt for the right planter to complement a collection of drought-tolerant plants, and this stone trough was perfect.

Lamb's ear and sempervivum (hen and chicks) are particularly well suited for dry conditions, making them a natural choice in this arrangement. Muscari was originally collected in the wilds of Turkey and Afghanistan so it, too, is conditioned to grow in an arid environment. There are some intriguing textural contrasts in this design as well. The hen and chick's thick, waxy rosettes are a nice foil to the soft, woolly leaves of the lamb's ear and the unruly muscari foliage creates the illusion of water pouring over the rock—another strong contrast.

The planter makes a strong addition to a grouping of similar rustic containers positioned together in a gravel mulch. It could also make a bold, solitary accent along a low stone wall.

Plant List
A. *'Helene Von Stein' lamb's ear*
B. *'Bewitched' dianthus*
C. *'Valerie Finnis' muscari*
D. *Hens and chicks*

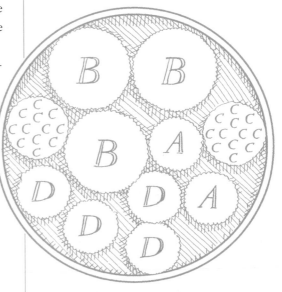

things to keep in mind
* Be careful not to overwater this planter. Good drainage is essential to the health and vitality of these plants; they don't like wet feet.
* Sempervivum will last for years in a container like this if given the right conditions.
* A single planting of sempervivum would also be striking, which may happen as the lamb's ear and dianthus pass through various growth stages and eventually fade.

PARTIAL SUN • Garden Home Principle: **ABUNDANCE**

II. Exuberant Stone Basket

Since this container is so visually rich, one is all you need to signal an exuberant welcome near the entry of your home. Create an asymmetrical display by pairing it with a large round boxwood or rose. The low and horizontal profile of this container allows full viewing of this robust display.

1   oval concrete planter—28 inches long × 20 inches wide × 12 inches deep
3   8-inch pots 'Sparkling Burgundy' pineapple lily (*Eucomis comosa* 'Sparkling Burgundy')
1   1-gallon purple creeping thrift (*Phlox subulata*)
1   1-gallon lavender creeping thrift (*Phlox subulata*)
2   1-gallon 'August Moon' hosta (*Hosta* 'August Moon')
3   1-quart 'Blueberry Sachet' nemesia (*Nemesia* × *hybrida* 'Blueberry Sachet')
3   1-quart 'Wildside' Sunscape daisy (*Osteospermum fruticosum* 'Wildside')
3   1-quart 'Seaside' Sunscape daisy (*Osteospermum fruticosum* 'Seaside')
3   1-quart 'Highside' Sunscape daisy (*Osteospermum fruticosum* 'Highside')
2   1-quart 'Oriental Limelight' artemisia (*Artemisia vulgaris* 'Oriental Limelight')
3   1-quart 'Metallic Blue' Outback daisy (*Brachyscome* 'Metallic Blue')

While snooping around the back of a rundown nursery I discovered this cast concrete container buried under a pile of empty pots. Upon unearthing it, I noticed it looked as though someone had used a woven basket for the mold. It already had a nice mossy patina and even though it was chipped, I thought it was good looking and had lots of potential.

The basket motif seems to be the right fit for a cheerful collection of osteospermums with their daisylike forms and rich, saturated colors. The chartreuse foliage of the 'Oriental Limelight' artemisia also helps to brighten the composition like a "live wire" that shows up at a party and gets it going, and nemesia and phlox are reliable container mates. Both help soften the edge of the container and round out the arrangement to give it a full, billowy look.

The secret to creating this basket of blooms is to start planting the eucomis in the center and then work out from there. Once you finish, integrate the foliage of the various plants. This technique helps make the arrangement appear as though the plants grew up together, giving the container a fully mature, gardenlike character.

Plant List

A. 'Sparkling Burgundy' pineapple lily
B. Purple creeping thrift
C. Lavender creeping thrift
D. 'August Moon' hosta
E. 'Blueberry Sachet' nemesia
F. 'Wildside' Sunscape daisy
G. 'Highside' Sunscape daisy
H. 'Seaside' Sunscape daisy
I. 'Oriental Limelight' artemisia
J. 'Metallic Blue' Outback daisy

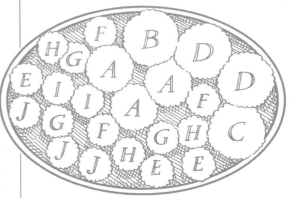

things to keep in mind

* Pincushion flowers or geraniums are good substitutes for osteospermum if they are not available in your area.
* Heavily planted containers can dry out quickly, so check them regularly.
* Be sure the planter has drainage holes before you begin planting.

'ORIENTAL LIMELIGHT' ARTEMISIA

'SPARKLING BURGUNDY' PINEAPPLE LILY

'SEASIDE' SUNSCAPE DAISY

'WILDSIDE' SUNSCAPE DAISY

'AUGUST MOON' HOSTA

'HIGHSIDE' SUNSCAPE DAISY

LAVENDER CREEPING THRIFT

'METALLIC BLUE' OUTBACK DAISY

'BLUEBERRY SACHET' NEMESIA

· No. 11 ·

rhythm

SUN • Garden Home Principle: **WHIMSY**

12. Spring Meadow in Painted Tub

Slapping a bright coat of paint on a galvanized tub is often all you need to do to turn an ordinary container into a treasured find. I couldn't resist transforming this hardware store purchase into a much better version of itself with some periwinkle blue paint. Couldn't you see this at the edge of a vegetable garden, or in a small garden room full of patio furniture with striped cushioned seats? Fill it with color-splashed plants and call it fun.

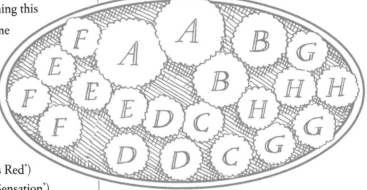

1   galvanized oval tub painted blue—
    22 inches long × 18 inches wide × 13 inches deep
2   1-gallon 'Huskers Red' penstemon (*Penstemon digitalis* 'Huskers Red')
2   8-inch pots 'Red Sensation' cordyline (*Cordyline australis* 'Red Sensation')
2   1-quart 'Sweet Kate' spiderwort (*Tradescantia* × *andersoniana* 'Sweet Kate')
3   1-quart purple heart (*Tradescantia pallida*)
3   1-quart 'Comet Pink' argyranthemum (*Argyranthemum frutescens* 'Comet Pink')
3   1-quart 'Lanai Royal Purple' verbena (*Verbena hybrida* 'Lanai Royal Purple')
3   1-quart Whispers 'Blue Rose' petunia (*Petunia hybrida* 'Blue Rose')
3   1-quart 'Seaside' Sunscape daisy (*Osteospermum fruticosum* 'Seaside')

Plant List
A. *'Huskers Red' penstemon*
B. *'Red Sensation' cordyline*
C. *'Sweet Kate' spiderwort*
D. *Purple heart*
E. *'Comet Pink' argyranthemum*
F. *'Lanai Royal Purple' verbena*
G. *Whispers 'Blue Rose' petunia*
H. *'Seaside' Sunscape daisy*

When I discovered this oval-shaped galvanized tub in a hardware store, I immediately recognized its hidden potential. Using brightly colored containers in a garden room sets a festive mood and playfully showcases a plant arrangement. One thing to keep in mind as you select plants for colorful containers is to mix together both foliage and flowering varieties. Sometimes it is hard to look past all the blooms in a garden center and focus on plants with great leaf color, but the resulting blend is a lot more interesting.

In this container the deep burgundy leaves of purple heart, 'Red Sensation' cordyline, and 'Huskers Red' penstemon flaunt their foliage against the bright flowers of the osteospermums, petunias, verbena, argyranthemums, and spiderwort. This rich mixture of saturated colors helps to balance the tub's vivid blue color, and adds visual weight that further anchors the plantings to the container.

things to keep in mind
* Drill holes in the bottom of the container for drainage.
* Use a paint designed to adhere to metal for a long-lasting finish.
* Be sure the container's outer surface is clean and dry before applying the paint.

'RED SENSATION' CORDYLINE

'HUSKERS RED' PENSTEMON

'SEASIDE' SUNSCAPE DAISY

'COMET PINK' ARGYRANTHEMUM

'LANAI ROYAL PURPLE' VERBENA

WHISPERS 'BLUE ROSE' PETUNIA

PURPLE HEART

'SWEET KATE' SPIDERWORT

No. 12

SUN • Garden Home Principle: **ENTRY**

13. Bouquet in Moss-Lined Lattice Urn

Depending on the occasion, this lattice urn can be dressed up or down. The design pictured here shows its fun and flirty side. Imagine it next to a metal bench, or as a focal point in a small garden room.

1   lattice mesh basket urn with moss—31 inches tall × 15 inches diameter with 18-inch basket)

2   large bags of sphagnum moss (presoak before use) or bags of sheet moss

1   dark garbage bag—cut to fit (poke holes in the bottom for drainage)

1   1-gallon 'Red Sensation' cordyline (*Cordyline australis* 'Red Sensation')

2   1-gallon 'Huskers Red' penstemon (*Penstemon digitalis* 'Huskers Red')

2   1-quart 'Helene Von Stein' lamb's ear (*Stachys byzantina* 'Helene Von Stein')

3   3-inch pots 'Rocky Mountain Light Pink' geranium (*Pelargonium* × *hortorum* 'Rocky Mountain Light Pink')

1   1-quart pot 'Glacier' English ivy (*Hedera helix* 'Glacier')

2   1-quart or 2 six-packs 'Super Parfait Raspberry' dianthus (*Dianthus chinensis* 'Super Parfait Raspberry')

When I discovered a pair of these lattice-mesh baskets in a shop, they reminded me of some I had seen in France years ago. I was eager to buy them because I knew without a doubt that I would use them in a million different ways in my garden. When I got them home, I immediately put them to work by lining them with sheet moss and a pliable garbage bag with drainage holes to hold the moss and soil in place. When I tried this without the liner, the moss broke loose in several places and soil spilled out of the basket. So if you don't use the bag as a liner, be generous with the moss and pack it in as tightly as possible.

The overall color theme of this arrangement is varying shades of pink. To display it in its full spectrum, three plants come into play. The dianthus represents the midcolor range, while the deeper tones are introduced by the penstemons and accented by the lighter geraniums. Using plants that share a common pigment from the same color family is always a safe and successful bet. The frosty gray 'Helene Von Stein' lamb's ear blends in well with the shades of pink. Its soft woolly leaves are larger than those of other lamb's ear varieties. Once the plants are all arranged, the container appears as though a tiny corner of a spring flower garden was dug up and dropped right into the basket.

Plant List

A. *'Red Sensation' cordyline*

B. *'Huskers Red' penstemon*

C. *'Helene Von Stein' lamb's ear*

D. *'Rocky Mountain Light Pink' geranium*

E. *'Glacier' English ivy*

F. *'Super Parfait Raspberry' dianthus*

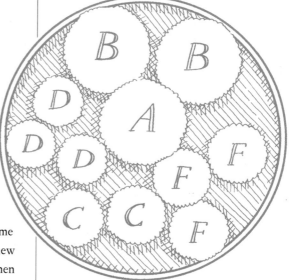

things to keep in mind

❉ The open weave of the urn allows the soil to dry out quickly, so check it regularly and keep the soil consistently moist.

❉ If displayed on a hard surface, the urn will need protection underneath to prevent staining from water drainage.

'SOUTHERN CHARM' ORNAMENTAL MULLEIN

'ORIGAMI YELLOW' COLUMBINE

'ORANIA PEACH' SUNSCAPE DAISY

STRAWBERRY BEGONIA

'GOLDEN BABY' IVY

'TOFFEE TWIST' SEDGE

'ANTIQUE ROSE' NEMESIA

· No. 14 ·

SUN • Garden Home Principle: **FRAME (OR SCREEN) A VIEW**

14. Cottage Garden Cluster

Staggered sizes of terra-cotta containers bursting with spring flowers create an instant cottage garden for a sunny location. Clustered pots can help hide unsightly or distracting elements in the garden such as water spigots, air-conditioning units, or coiled hoses. Groupings are also effective ways of anchoring a corner of a terrace or signaling a transition between two different areas of the garden.

3   round terra-cotta containers
    • Large container—15 inches diameter × 13 inches deep
    • Medium container—14 inches diameter × 12 inches deep
    • Small container—12 inches diameter × 6 inches deep

LARGE CONTAINER

3   1-quart 'Origami Yellow' columbine (*Aquilegia caerulea* 'Origami Yellow')
1   1-gallon 'Antique Rose' nemesia (*Nemesia caerulea* hybrid 'Antique Rose')
3   1-quart 'Orania Peach' Sunscape daisy (*Osteospermum ecklonis* 'Orania Peach')
1   1-quart 'Toffee Twist' sedge (*Carex flagellifera* 'Toffee Twist')
1   1-quart strawberry begonia (*Saxifraga stolonifera*)
1   1-quart 'Golden Baby' ivy (*Hedera helix* 'Golden Baby')

MEDIUM CONTAINER

4   1-gallon 'Southern Charm' ornamental mullein (*Verbascum × hybrida* 'Southern Charm')

SMALL CONTAINER

2   1-gallon 'Antique Rose' nemesia (*Nemesia caerulea* hybrid 'Antique Rose')

Okay, so maybe the idea of using brown grass ('Toffee Twist' sedge) in a spring container seems a little strange. But just look at the results! The fun of this arrangement is its focus on unusual plants, like the carex and verbascum 'Southern Charm'.

The refined colors in this combination look best against a dark, contrasting background such as a walnut-stained fence or a building with dark siding. The color of the terra-cotta pots keeps the grouping light, preserving the harmony of the arrangement.

After the verbascum and columbine finish their spring bloom, they can be moved into the garden, leaving the grass and nemesia in place as the basis for a brand-new summer container.

Plant List
A. 'Origami Yellow' columbine
B. 'Antique Rose' nemesia
C. 'Orania Peach' Sunscape daisy
D. 'Toffee Twist' sedge
E. Strawberry begonia
F. 'Golden Baby' ivy
G. 'Southern Charm' ornamental mullein

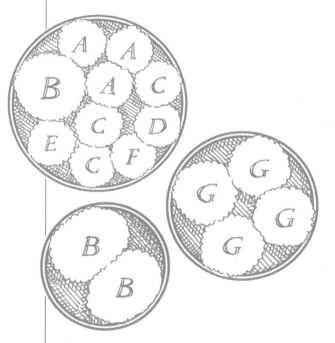

things to keep in mind
* Vary pot sizes for added visual interest.
* Experiment with specialty plants.
* After plants have flowered, substitute with fresh blooming varieties of similar forms: for the columbine, a soft buttery colored lantana, and for the tall vertical verbascum, *Salvia farinacea* 'Blue Victoria'.

SUMMeR

When summer is in full swing and my perennials and annuals are bursting with blooms, I finally have the chance to evaluate the results of some of my planting experiments. One of my favorite gardening pleasures is using containers as mini-laboratories to try out new combinations of plants. Each season brings a new world of possibilities and surprises.

I T IS SUCH A THRILL TO MIX UP A NEW BATCH OF CONTAINER PLANTS. ONE YEAR I MAY TRY AN OLD STANDBY LIKE THE PETUNIA ALONG WITH SOMETHING MORE EXOTIC LIKE LEMON-GRASS AND PURPLE HOT PEPPERS MIXED IN A CONTAINER. OR FOR A CHANGE, I MAY DECIDE TO WORK IN AN ENTIRELY DIFFERENT COLOR FAMILY THAN THE ONE I USED THE YEAR BEFORE. THIS WAY OF THINKING KEEPS ME ON THE LOOKOUT FOR INTERESTING PLANTS WHEREVER I GO.

Summer is the season that supports trial and error in the garden, especially in container designs. I find that nature is so forgiving. I can plant something, pull it out, replace it with something else, and within a few days the plants are growing again with the exuberance of the season.

Bubbling over with blooms, a carefree blend of 'Imperial Blue' plumbago, bouvardia, tropical hibiscus, 'Dove Wing's Patriot' lantana, and 'Blue Daze' evolvulus captures the spirit of a summer meadow.

I love the challenge of putting together new combinations of container plants hoping for a magical blend of colors, shapes, and textures that will successfully grow all summer long. This approach to container design appeals to my artistic nature as well as my botanical curiosity. As the plants evolve through summer, entwined in a dynamic embrace, I feel as though I am watching a painting develop right before my eyes.

There is a timeless feel to long summer days; they have an open-ended and expansive quality. Summer makes it seem that almost anything is possible. It's a wonderful time to create your own container experiments.

'RED SENSATION' CORDYLINE

'LEILANI BLUE' AGERATUM

'SALSA LIGHT PURPLE' SALVIA

'SALSA PURPLE' SALVIA

STAINED GLASSWORKS 'FRIGHT NIGHT' COLEUS

WHISPERS 'BLUE ROSE' PETUNIA

· No. 15 ·

15. Exuberant, Full-Sun Color

If you enjoy vibrant colors, this arrangement is for you. Bold and beautiful, it is an eye-catching focal point in any well-lit location. Place it near a cabana with flowering bougainvillea or, better still, display it along the edge of a swimming pool where the container mirrors the color of the pool's glazed tile.

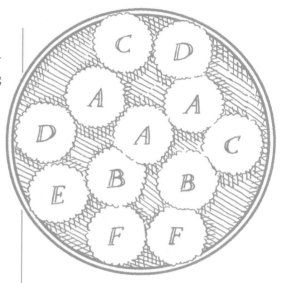

1	blue two-toned glazed ceramic container— 19 inches diameter × 11 inches deep
3	1-quart 'Red Sensation' cordyline (*Cordyline australis* 'Red Sensation')
2	1-quart 'Leilani Blue' ageratum (*Ageratum houstonianum* 'Leilani Blue')
2	1-quart Stained Glassworks 'Fright Night' coleus (*Solenostemon scutellariodes* 'Fright Night')
2	1-quart 'Salsa Light Purple' salvia (*Salvia splendens* 'Salsa Light Purple')
1	1-quart 'Salsa Purple' salvia (*Salvia splendens* 'Salsa Purple')
2	1-quart Whispers 'Blue Rose' petunia (*Petunia hybrida* 'Blue Rose')

Plant List
A. 'Red Sensation' cordyline
B. 'Leilani Blue' ageratum
C. Stained Glassworks 'Fright Night' coleus
D. 'Salsa Light Purple' salvia
E. 'Salsa Purple' salvia
F. Whispers 'Blue Rose' petunia

The vibrant colors of the plants in this arrangement work well with the deep blue of the glazed jardinière. 'Fright Night' coleus plays a big role in jazzing things up with its incredible colors.

If you are ever at a loss deciding which plants to combine in a container, just take a petal from a flower or even a single leaf from a plant like 'Fright Night' and use it as a guide. Hold it up against other possible choices to find plants that echo those colors. It's the easiest way I know to come up with color schemes that feel natural and fit comfortably in the landscape. Picking colors shouldn't be a trying experience. It should be fun, so just take your lead from nature.

After a few weeks, as the plants in this arrangement settle in, the 'Fright Night' coleus takes off and, living up to its name, seems to swallow the entire container. Coleus has a tendency to become a container thug. By simply pinching it back regularly, you can make the plant a bit less spooky.

things to keep in mind

※ Edit the coleus. It can be pushy and insensitive to its fellow container mates.

※ Remove spent flowers.

※ Part of this container's sassy attitude comes from its rich saturated colors. Remember, the bolder the contrast, the more attitude.

SUN • Garden Home Principle: **COLOR**

16. Salmon Bouquet in Green Water Jar

Become your own garden home "exterior designer" by extending the color scheme from your home's interior décor outdoors using color-coordinated plants and containers. Imagine sitting in a room decorated in shades of salmon and green with this planter displayed just outside on the patio or deck. By integrating exterior plants with your interior colors, you build a visual connection between both realms.

1	green ceramic water jar—19 inches diameter × 16 inches deep
2	1-gallon 'Victoria Blue' salvia (*Salvia farinacea* 'Victoria Blue')
2	1-quart Stained Glassworks 'Tilt a Whirl' coleus (*Solenostemon scutellariodes* 'Tilt a Whirl')
3	1-quart 'Picante Salmon' salvia (*Salvia splendens* 'Picante Salmon')
1	1-quart 'Evergold' sedge (*Carex hachijoensis* 'Evergold')
2	1-quart golden creeping Jenny (*Lysimachia nummularia* 'Aurea')

Plant List

A. *'Victoria Blue' salvia*
B. *Stained Glassworks 'Tilt a Whirl' coleus*
C. *'Picante Salmon' salvia*
D. *'Evergold' sedge*
E. *Golden creeping Jenny*

With so many great shapes and colors playing off one another, the plants in this container make a beautiful presentation. The strong contrast between the thin flowing leaves of 'Evergold' sedge and the broader, dark green foliage of 'Picante Salmon' salvia heightens the arrangement's visual interest. The color contrasts are also appealing with the chartreuse, salmon, and yellow leaves of 'Tilt a Whirl' coleus against the vertical violet-blue flower spikes of 'Victoria Blue' salvia.

Building color harmony as well as contrast is important in order to make the composition feel balanced. For example, the 'Tilt a Whirl' coleus leaves pick up both the chartreuse tinge in creeping Jenny's foliage and the yellow tones in the 'Evergold' sedge unifying the composition.

If the colors in this container don't match those in your home's interior, another way to display this planter is to place it in a flower border. The presentation is especially effective when it appears to emerge out of a bed planted en masse with 'Evergold' sedge.

things to keep in mind

❋ Creeping Jenny will certainly live up to its name, so if you provide a toehold along the edge of the pot, it will spill over the side, opening up room in the container for other plants.

❋ Pinch back the spent blossoms of the salvia to encourage new blooms.

❋ Transplant perennials into flowerbeds late in the season so you can enjoy them again next year.

things to keep in mind
* Tropical plants add drama to herbaceous borders and containers.
* This container does best with morning sun and afternoon shade, especially when the temperatures turn hot.
* Don't forget to keep the container well watered.

PARTIAL SHADE • Garden Home Principle: **SHAPE AND FORM**

17. 'Black Magic' Surprise

Set a tropical mood with this container by combining it with some rattan and bamboo furniture. The wind loves to play with the large leaves of the 'Black Magic' elephant's ear, giving the container an entrancing sense of movement and bringing a spirit of the exotic to your garden.

1   pale green clay pot—18 inches diameter × 15 inches deep
1   1-gallon 'Concord Grape' spiderwort (*Tradescantia × andersoniana* 'Concord Grape')
3   1-quart 'Black Magic' elephant's ear (*Colocasia esculenta* 'Black Magic')
1   1-gallon 'Morning Light' miscanthus (*Miscanthus sinensis* 'Morning Light')
1   1-gallon 'Hermann's Pride' lamiastrum (*Lamiastrum galeobdolon* 'Hermann's Pride')
2   1-quart 'Duchess Deep Blue' torenia (*Torenia fournieri* 'Duchess Deep Blue')
3   1-quart purple heart (*Tradescantia pallida*)
1   1-quart 'Glacier' English ivy (*Hedera helix* 'Glacier')

Foliar drama can be heightened in a container with the addition of tropical plants. I grew elephant ears as a child and I always thought it was great fun to load the plants with fertilizer to see how big an "ear" I could grow! There is no question that these exotic, large-leafed plants are real standouts, especially when they are paired with smaller, more delicate foliage.

In this arrangement, the plant definitely commands attention. Its sooty, dark purple leaves can grow nearly two feet long and the plant itself can stretch up to five feet. For contrast, two plants with narrow blades, 'Concord Grape' spiderwort and miscanthus grass, add a touch of the African savannah to the arrangement. 'Duchess Deep Blue' torenia makes a color bridge to the bright blue blossoms of the spiderwort. Purple heart tumbles over the edge and creates a cascading element along the rim of the container, its dark leaves repeating the shadowy hues in 'Black Magic'. The plum and silver mix of the plants blends well with the silvery green cast of the container.

The result is so dramatic that you will want to place it in a prominent place that is clearly visible from the interior of your home, perhaps near a window where you can catch a glimpse of it as you watch a rerun of *The African Queen* with Bogart and Hepburn!

Plant List
A. *'Concord Grape' spiderword*
B. *'Black Magic' elephant's ear*
C. *'Morning Light' miscanthus*
D. *'Hermann's Pride' lamiastrum*
E. *'Duchess Deep Blue' torenia*
F. *Purple heart*
G. *'Glacier' English ivy*

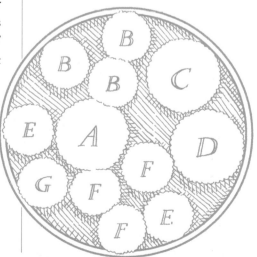

18. Chartreuse and Blue Full-Sun Container

Sparks of acid green electrify this arrangement and keep it from becoming a moody, tranquil combination. This container makes a great accent for a front door or garden gate, especially if the entrance is painted bright blue or purple.

1	blue square drip-glaze ceramic container— 19 inches × 19 inches × 19 inches tall
1	8-inch pot 'Royal Candles' veronica (*Veronica spicata* 'Royal Candles')
3	1-gallon Mexican feather grass (*Nassella tenuissina*)
1	8 to 10-inch hanging basket 'Purple Moon' torenia (*Torenia fournieri* hybrid 'Purple Moon')
1	1-gallon 'Ogon' sedum (*Sedum makinoi* 'Ogon')
1	1-quart 'Duchess Light Blue' torenia (*Torenia fournieri* 'Duchess Light Blue')
1	1-quart 'Rachel's Gold' salvia (*Salvia officinalis* 'Rachel's Gold')

I found myself scratching my head over what colors to use in this arrangement in order to balance the container's vivid blue color. Then it hit me. Chartreuse! It's a daring color, not for the faint of heart. You have to have a spirit of adventure in order to use it, but once you do, you'll find it offers great rewards.

'Ogon' sedum's mound of yellow-green foliage works perfectly as the focal point of the design. It is irresistible with its springy mat of tiny golden leaves that seem to bubble up from the corner of the container. It is a vigorous grower that performs unflinchingly during summer's inferno.

The bright, electric green leaves of 'Rachel's Gold' salvia builds on the chartreuse theme and adds just the right accent of color, especially when combined with the bright green blades of the Mexican feather grass. The blue and purple blooms of the torenias help give the medley some depth and echo the colors in the container. Together they create a lively balance of foliage and blooms.

This container demonstrates how using my Three-Shape Rule helps to economize the available space in a planter. Tall and spiky plants grow upward, round and full ones grow outward, and cascading plants spill over the side. Each plant form fills in different areas of the container, allowing you to work with a broad range of shapes.

Plant List

A. 'Royal Candles' veronica
B. Mexican feather grass
C. 'Purple Moon' torenia
D. 'Ogon' sedum
E. 'Duchess Light Blue' torenia
F. 'Rachel's Gold' salvia

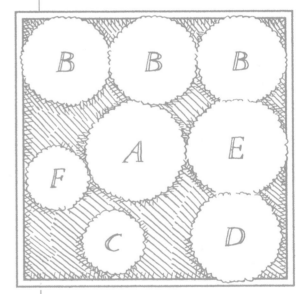

things to keep in mind

* As summer winds down, transplant the perennials into the garden.
* Remove spent blooms of veronica to encourage more flowers.
* Showcase unusual plants by placing them alongside plants of contrasting color and form—in this case the torenia helps to frame the 'Ogon' sedum.

PARTIAL SUN • Garden Home Principle: **STRUCTURE**

19. Clematis and Geraniums in a Trellised Box

Here's a chance to start thinking outside the box. Place this trellised container on a large table to dress up a blank wall, or if you prefer, keep it at ground level and use a series of these boxes to define the edge of a garden area to help provide a degree of privacy.

1   box with faux lead finish—33 inches long × 17 inches wide × 14 inches deep

1   painted wooden trellis—32 inches long × 31 inches tall above the soil

1   2-gallon lavender clematis (*Clematis* hybrid)

4   1-quart Persian shield (*Strobilanthes dyerianus*)

5   1-quart 'Bravo' geranium (*Pelargonium* × *hortorum* 'Bravo')

4   1-quart golden creeping Jenny (*Lysimachia nummularia* 'Aurea')

4   1-quart 'Bronze Beauty' ajuga (*Ajuga reptans* 'Bronze Beauty')

As a designer, one challenge is to find room for a garden in areas with limited space. Often the solution is found in using trellises and walls to create vertical gardens.

Adding a trellis to the back of this container is a great way to add a sense of structure. The design of the trellis can echo a home's architecture. A twig trellis matches a rustic-style home, and a fan-shape trellis wonderfully complements a Victorian home.

The lavender clematis in this arrangement eagerly scampers up the trellis, filling the support with beautiful blooms. Abundant rosy pink blooms of 'Bravo' geraniums also brighten the container. The flowers add a nice round and full shape to the composition. The leaves of the Persian shield have a lavender and pink sheen that is repeated in the pink geraniums and the lavender blossoms of the clematis. As a finishing touch, the bronzy green leaves of the ajuga and the lime green strands of the creeping Jenny spill over the edge in an appealing mix of color.

The geraniums bloom on and off throughout the summer (responding well to regular feedings) and display renewed signs of vigor as autumn approaches and temperatures cool down. Deadheading the spent blossoms encourages new buds, and pinching back the Persian shield keeps the container balanced. This design is perfect for the apartment dweller or homeowner who has a small area that gets morning sun and afternoon shade.

Plant List

A. *Lavender clematis*

B. *Persian shield*

C. *'Bravo' geranium*

D. *Golden creeping Jenny*

E. *'Bronze Beauty' ajuga*

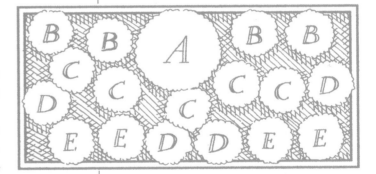

things to keep in mind

* To create the illusion of depth in a container, use a medley of dark and light foliage plants. If all of the leaves are the same color, the arrangement appears flat and one-dimensional.

* As the clematis climbs, use green garden twine to tie the vine to the trellis. It is almost invisible and guides the growth of the plant.

* Make sure the size of the trellis matches the scale of the container.

SHADE • Garden Home Principle: **ABUNDANCE**

20. Shade-Loving Tabletop Centerpiece

Bringing your favorite plants together in one container is like inviting several of your closest friends to a party. The chemistry is often pleasantly surprising. This combination is proof that it works. Use it as a centerpiece for an outdoor dining room. Its low profile means that it won't obstruct a view, but it is prominent enough to get noticed.

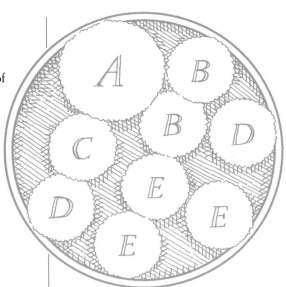

1   green ceramic bowl—18 inches diameter × 8 inches deep
1   1-gallon society garlic (*Tulbaghia violacea*)
2   1-quart 'Party Time' Joseph's coat (*Alternanthera ficoidea* 'Party Time')
1   1-quart 'Chameleon' euphorbia (*Euphorbia dulcis* 'Chameleon')
2   1-quart variegated Cuban oregano (*Plectranthus amboinicus*)
3   1-quart 'Sonic Light Pink' New Guinea impatiens (*Impatiens × hybrida* 'Sonic Light Pink')

This container is designed to overflow with visual abundance, creating a stunning centerpiece that lasts for a long time. The soft, luminous pink blooms of the New Guinea impatiens churn out all summer as the three foliage plants chime in with more color. The broody 'Chameleon' euphorbia, white variegated Cuban oregano, and the appropriately named 'Party Time' Joseph's coat each add their own element of color, pattern, and texture to the pink impatiens. Society garlic holds an unassuming position in the background, with its long grassy leaves, until it pushes out spikes of lavender flowers that take flight and bloom for several weeks.

The neutral color of the container blends easily with the plants' color palette. Because of its size, the arrangement is easily moved, so it can be displayed in many places.

things to keep in mind
⁕ Low bowls are good for outdoor dining centerpieces.
⁕ When you are generous with plants in a container, keep up with their watering and feeding needs.

Plant List
A. *Society garlic*
B. *'Party Time' Joseph's coat*
C. *'Chameleon' euphorbia*
D. *Variegated Cuban oregano*
E. *'Sonic Light Pink' New Guinea impatiens*

SOCIETY GARLIC

'PARTY TIME' JOSEPH'S COAT

'CHAMELEON' EUPHORBIA

VARIEGATED CUBAN OREGANO

'SONIC LIGHT PINK' NEW GUINEA IMPATIENS

· No. 20 ·

SUN • Garden Home Principle: **COLOR**

21. Ivy Geranium and Coleus in Campana Pot

This cheerful arrangement adds a delightful accent to a casual border along a picket fence or near a gated entrance to the garden. Bursting with color, the plants perform beautifully all summer.

- 1 round campana terra-cotta pot—21 inches diameter × 15 inches deep
- 2 1-gallon purple fountain grass (*Pennisetum setaceum* 'Rubrum')
- 3 1-quart 'Carlos' lantana (*Lantana camara* 'Carlos')
- 2 1-quart 'Limelight' licorice plant (*Helichrysum petiolare* 'Limelight')
- 1 8- to 10-inch hanging basket 'Molina' ivy geranium (*Pelargonium* × *peltatum* 'Molina')
- 1 1-gallon Stained Glassworks 'Swiss Sunshine' coleus (*Solenostemon scutellariodes* 'Swiss Sunshine')
- 1 1-quart 'Ramblin' Peach Glo' petunia (*Petunia hybrida* 'Ramblin' Peach Glo')

I recall on my first trip to Europe how surprised I was by the prolific use of flowers. There were flowers planted everywhere! I was particularly impressed with the gorgeous window boxes in Italy and France that were filled with annuals spilling over the sides. Over and over again I saw ivy geraniums as a prominent feature in the designs and I was determined to find some when I returned home. With this design, I made use of these memories.

Here, the stage is set with a showy variety called 'Molina'. Her double salmon pink blooms shower the container in color. 'Ramblin' Peach Glo' petunia repeats the geranium's performance with its own impressive display. Another star performer in this collection of plants is 'Swiss Sunshine' coleus. Even during the brutal heat of summer, it supplies nonstop color with its green, pink, and pale yellow foliage. Also a standout in the bunch is 'Carlos' lantana, with its fiery red-purple blooms with orange and gold centers, which eagerly pick up the slack when the geraniums slow down in midsummer. Much like all of us, the ivy geraniums appreciate some afternoon shade as the temperatures climb.

things to keep in mind

- If your planting looks a bit unbalanced, try setting a smaller companion pot next to the large container to help the composition look more proportional.
- Remove spent flowers from the ivy geranium to encourage more blooms.
- Pinch back plants as they grow to keep the arrangement from looking unruly.

Plant List

A. *Purple fountain grass*
B. *'Carlos' lantana*
C. *'Limelight' licorice plant*
D. *'Molina' ivy geranium*
E. *Stained Glassworks 'Swiss Sunshine' coleus*
F. *'Ramblin' Peach Glo' petunia*

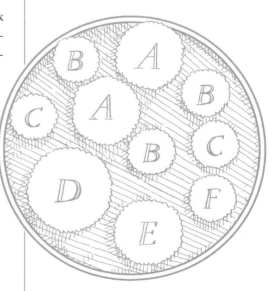

PURPLE FOUNTAIN GRASS

'CARLOS' LANTANA

'MOLINA' IVY GERANIUM

'LIMELIGHT' LICORICE PLANT

STAINED GLASSWORKS 'SWISS SUNSHINE' COLEUS

'RAMBLIN' PEACH GLO' PETUNIA

• No. 21 •

'ORIENTAL LIMELIGHT' ARTEMESIA

'RED SENSATION' CORDYLINE

LAVENDER PENTAS

PERSIAN SHIELD

'RACHEL'S GOLD' SALVIA

GANGES PRIMROSE

'DUCHESS LIGHT BLUE' TORENIA

'CASCADIAS IMPROVED CHARLIE' PETUNIA

• No. 22 •

SUN • Garden Home Principle: **TEXTURE, PATTERN, AND RHYTHM**

22. Persian Shield Sensation

Several of these containers placed rhythmically through a flower border make a striking statement. Their generous size gives newly established gardens instant structure and visual mass until larger plants fill in. They can also help to soften the look of a privacy fence.

1 terra-cotta container—22 inches diameter × 20 inches deep

1 1-gallon 'Red Sensation' cordyline (*Cordyline australis* 'Red Sensation')

3 1-quart Persian shield (*Strobilanthes dyerianus*)

3 1-quart lavender pentas (*Pentas lanceolata*)

3 1-quart 'Oriental Limelight' artemisia (*Artemisia vulgaris* 'Oriental Limelight')

3 1-quart 'Cascadias Improved Charlie' petunia (*Petunia hybrida* 'Cascadias Improved Charlie')

3 1-quart Ganges primrose (*Asystasia gangetica*)

2 1-quart 'Rachel's Gold' salvia (*Salvia officinalis* 'Rachel's Gold')

2 1-quart 'Duchess Light Blue' torenia (*Torenia fournieri* 'Duchess Light Blue')

Big and bold is what this design is all about. I had an old terra-cotta container in the potting shed just begging to be planted so I headed to the garden center to see what I could find. When I spied the striking metallic purple foliage of the Persian shield, I wanted to give it a starring role in the composition. The bronzy red blades of 'Red Sensation' cordyline play off the rich foliage of the Persian shield and the dark hues of the clay container.

 To keep the color scheme from becoming too somber, the bright green foliage of 'Oriental Limelight' and 'Rachel's Gold' salvia adds some pizzazz. To echo the purple, green, and gold color theme of the foliage plants, lavender pentas, 'Duchess Light Blue' torenia, 'Cascadias Improved Charlie' petunia, and Ganges primrose add their own flower power. The Ganges primrose is a little-known plant from the tropics that is destined to become quite popular. It is a vigorous groundcover with bell-shaped flowers ranging from pale yellow to pink that works well in the container as a trailing element.

Plant List

A. 'Red Sensation' cordyline

B. Persian shield

C. Lavender pentas

D. 'Oriental Limelight' artemesia

E. 'Cascadias Improved Charlie' petunia

F. Ganges primrose

G. 'Rachel's Gold' salvia

H. 'Duchess Light Blue' torenia

things to keep in mind

✳ Many of these plants are robust and need to be regularly snipped back into bounds. The artemisia, Persian shield, petunias, and Ganges primrose respond well to the knife and become bushier and more evenly shaped when pruned.

✳ By late summer the performance of the torenia and the salvia declines, most likely due to overcrowding by its more vigorous container mates.

SUN • Garden Home Principle: **ENTRY**

23. Classic Salmon Geraniums and Angelonia

For someone with just a sliver of space who longs for the beauty of a lush garden, this charming container makes a wonderful adornment for a doorstep or walkway. The ball-shaped container is reminiscent of a finial, making it a complementary feature to a home's railing or fence.

1   round terra-cotta pot (aged by mixing dove-gray latex paint with water [9 to 1], apply by dabbing it on the exterior with a damp cloth or sponge)—14 inches diameter × 14 inches deep

1   1-gallon purple fountain grass (*Pennisetum setaceum* 'Rubrum')

2   1-gallon 'Rocky Mountain Salmon' geranium (*Pelargonium × hortorum* 'Rocky Mountain Salmon')

2   1-quart 'Carita Purple' angelonia (*Angelonia angustifolia* 'Carita Purple')

1   1-quart 'Limelight' licorice plant (*Helichrysum petiolare* 'Limelight')

Plant List
A. *Purple fountain grass*
B. *'Rocky Mountain Salmon' geranium*
C. *'Carita Purple' angelonia*
D. *'Limelight' licorice plant*

Classic terra-cotta is usually my first choice in containers. Regardless of their size or shape, they are a natural fit in nearly every garden setting. The rounded bowl of this terra-cotta container caught my eye, so I wanted to find a plant with a flower form to repeat that shape. The ball-shaped blooms of the 'Rocky Mountain Salmon' geraniums filled the order beautifully.

When it comes to choosing plants, I often like to set up a bit of drama between color families by selecting opposites on the color wheel. With this composition, I began with 'Carita Purple' angelonia drawn from the blue/purple area of the wheel and then introduced a softened shade of salmon geraniums from the opposite side. A bright green patch of 'Limelight' licorice plant in the front of the urn helps to shake things up. The tall spiky blades at the back of the planter are purple fountain grass. The blades lengthen during the season and are a prominent element in the container, particularly as the soft burgundy seed heads emerge.

things to keep in mind

✳ To soften the color of the terra-cotta pot, dab the outer surface with a diluted solution of soft gray latex paint. Then rub the surface with a cloth to give it a well-worn look.

✳ For a mossy green patina, rub handfuls of green weeds on the surface.

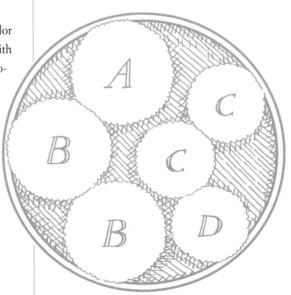

things to keep in mind

* Match the color of your containers to colors in the area where they will be displayed.
* Pinch back aggressive plants to keep the composition in balance.

24. Cool Duo for Summer Sun

Get the party going on your deck or patio. Start with some bold striped cushions for your patio furniture, throw in a brightly colored umbrella, and then add these fabulously festive containers. Don't forget the margaritas!

1 round turquoise ceramic container—20 inches diameter × 15 inches deep
1 turquoise-glazed strawberry jar—8 inches diameter × 15 inches deep

LARGE CONTAINER

3 1-quart 'Purple Majesty' ornamental millet (*Pennisetum glaucum* 'Purple Majesty')
2 1-quart 'Black and Blue' salvia (*Salvia guaranitica* 'Black and Blue')
2 1-quart 'Imperial Blue' plumbago (*Plumbago auriculata* 'Imperial Blue')
3 1-quart 'Limelight' licorice plant (*Helichrysum petiolare* 'Limelight')
2–3 1-quart 'Reflections Lavender' petunia (*Petunia hybrida* 'Reflections Lavender')
2–3 1-quart 'Cascadias Improved Charlie' petunia (*Petunia hybrida* 'Cascadias Improved Charlie')

STRAWBERRY JAR

1 1-quart 'Ogon' sedum (*Sedum makinoi* 'Ogon')
1 1-quart parrot's beak (*Lotus berthelotii*)
1 1-quart 'Reflections Lavender' petunia (*Petunia hybrida* 'Reflections Lavender')
1 1-quart 'Limelight' licorice plant (*Helichrysum petiolare* 'Limelight')
1 1-quart 'Silver Spike' helichrysum (*Helichrysum thianschanicum* 'Silver Spike')
1 6-pack—2 plugs 'Purple Robe' cupflower (*Nierembergia frutescens* 'Purple Robe')
1 6-pack—3 plugs 'Margarita Pink' moss rose (*Portulaca grandiflora* 'Margarita Pink')

Plant List

A. 'Purple Majesty' ornamental millet
B. 'Black and Blue' salvia
C. 'Imperial Blue' plumbago
D. 'Limelight' licorice plant
E. 'Reflections Lavender' petunia
F. 'Cascadias Improved Charlie' petunia
G. 'Ogon' sedum
H. Parrot's beak
I. 'Silver Spike' helichrysum
J. 'Purple Robe' cupflower
K. 'Margarita Pink' moss rose

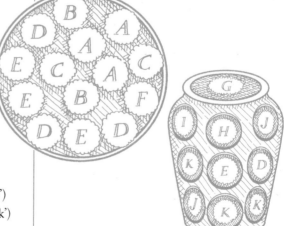

"Plays well with others" is the description I would give to this plant collection. Its pleasing palette of green, blue, purple, and a healthy dose of burgundy offers a range of colors that can easily be picked up in the fabric, furniture, and accessories on a patio or deck.

'Purple Majesty' millet, the tallest element in the arrangement, is an annual that can be grown from seed and then transplanted into the pot, or it can be purchased at the garden center ready to plant. In its early stages 'Purple Majesty' is mostly green, and then with maturity and full sun, it transforms into a wonderful shade of dark purple. In its prime, it can be nearly four feet high with flower spikes that are a foot long. As the seed heads dance in the wind, the millet adds a nice element of movement to the design.

The 'Black and Blue' salvia, which grows to several feet, needs to be regularly pinched back to stay out of the millet's territory. The salvia's waves of dark blue flowers are good companions to the light blue flower clusters of the 'Imperial Blue' plumbago. The dependable 'Cascadias Improved Charlie' petunia fills in the lower areas of the container with its dark purple blooms. Its flowers play among the felty green leaves of the helichrysum and the blooms of the lavender petunia.

To help balance the height of the millet, the large container can be paired with a strawberry jar in the same bright blue color filled with plants that echo those in the lower areas of the large container.

SUN/PARTIAL SHADE • Garden Home Principle: **ENCLOSURE**

25. 'General Sikorsky' Clematis Combo

Start with a terra-cotta container, add a wooden trellis, and you've created a flowering screen for a porch or patio anywhere you need a little privacy. The added height also provides a bit of filtered shade. Placing two or more containers along the edge of a seating area allows for even more coverage.

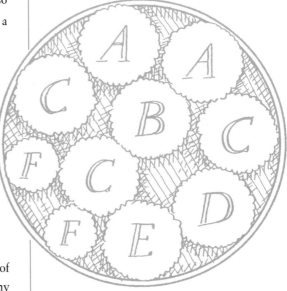

1	roll-rim terra-cotta container—18 inches diameter × 17 inches deep
1	wooden trellis painted green—37 inches wide × 37 inches tall
2	1-gallon 'General Sikorsky' clematis (*Clematis* 'General Sikorsky')
1	1-gallon 'Variegatus' Japanese silver grass (*Miscanthus sinensis* 'Variegatus')
3	1-gallon 'Victoria Blue' salvia (*Salvia farinacea* 'Victoria Blue')
1	1-gallon 'Hermann's Pride' lamiastrum (*Lamiastrum galeobdolon* 'Hermann's Pride')
1	1-gallon 'Purple Moon' torenia (*Torenia fournieri* hybrid 'Purple Moon')
2	1-quart variegated Cuban oregano (*Plectranthus amboinicus*)

It's no wonder that clematis are known as the "Queen of the Vines." I am a big fan of these climbing beauties and look for every opportunity to integrate them into my designs. Because of their ability to scamble up vertical surfaces, they are perfect for bringing visual interest to a trellis or wall.

A blue clematis, 'General Sikorsky' lends a serene accent to this arrangement. This variety is a fairly recent introduction (1980) that lives up to its reputation as a good repeat bloomer by producing waves of blossoms several times during the course of the summer. The flower's blue color is mirrored in the 'Purple Moon' torenia tumbling down the front of the container. Japanese silver grass erupts from the center to give the composition a lift. The white accents in the grass are repeated in the variegated leaves of the Cuban oregano and in the shiny silver and green veined foliage of 'Hermann's Pride' lamiastrum. To help balance the size and scale of the large trellised container, a smaller terra-cotta pot full of billowy 'Hermann's Pride' lamiastrum can be placed next to it.

things to keep in mind

* Trellised containers offer instant privacy to any location.
* Perennials such as clematis, Japanese silver grass, 'Victoria Blue' salvia, and lamiastrum can be used as container plants for a season and then transplanted to a more permanent spot for the future.
* In the hottest months of summer the lamiastrums enjoy afternoon shade and consistent moisture.

Plant List

A. *'General Sikorsky' clematis*
B. *'Variegatus' Japanese silver grass*
C. *'Victoria Blue' salvia*
D. *'Hermann's Pride' lamiastrum*
E. *'Purple Moon' torenia*
F. *Variegated Cuban oregano*

SHADE • Garden Home Principle: **FOCAL POINT**

26. Fern and White Flax Lily Centerpiece

Why not create a living centerpiece you can enjoy all summer? This container is the perfect size for an outdoor dining table.

1   round white fluted ceramic container—
      12 inches diameter (10-inch opening) × 10 inches deep
1   1-quart variegated flax lily (*Dianella tasmanica* 'Variegata')
1   1-quart Japanese painted fern (*Athyrium niponicum* var. 'Pictum')
2   1-quart 'Silhouette Appleblossom' double impatiens
      (*Impatiens walleriana* 'Silhouette Appleblossom')
1   4-inch pot 'Pee Vee Cee' English ivy (*Hedera helix* 'Pee Vee Cee')
1   1-quart purple heart (*Tradescantia pallida*)

Plant List
A. Variegated flax lily
B. Japanese painted fern
C. 'Silhouette Appleblossom' double impatiens
D. 'Pee Vee Cee' English ivy
E. Purple heart

The curves and fluting of this lovely bowl had so much appeal that I wanted to find an especially charismatic arrangement of plants to complement its style. The little charmer among this ensemble is 'Appleblossom' double impatiens with its fluffy shell pink blooms set at the center of the container. The flowers look like pearls found in a seashell. The dazzling blooms always attract attention and admiration from garden guests seated at my outdoor dining table.

A small-leafed ivy dances along the edge of the container while variegated flax lily emerges from the back with its straplike leaves in stripes of green and white. The artful, silvery gray fronds of the Japanese painted fern add a lacy quality to the display. Its reddish highlights are echoed in the dark purple foliage of purple heart, making it a complete and satisfying composition.

things to keep in mind
* Place the container in a location with moderate morning sun to stimulate continuous blooms on the impatiens.
* Even moisture and well-drained soil are important to the vitality of the plants.

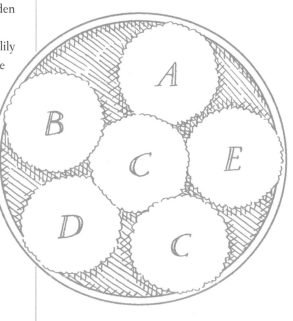

'ACCENT CORAL' IMPATIENS

'KIMBERLY QUEEN' FERN

'EVERGOLD' SEDGE

'FLORIDA SWEETHEART' CALADIUM

· No. 27 ·

SHADE • Garden Home Principle: **FOCAL POINT**

27. Caladium Spray in Urn

This is one container that won't sit in the background, demure and unnoticed. It is so tall and dramatic that one urn is all you need to make an unforgettable accent for your home's entrance. The distinctive outline of the floral trumpet-shaped urn and the hand-painted quality of the 'Florida Sweetheart' caladiums seem well suited for a situation where there is some distance between the container and the viewer, such as on a landing or at the end of a walkway, so one has the chance to appreciate the artistry of the design from afar.

1   metal urn—32 inches tall × 24 inches deep (with 12-inch planter diameter)
1   2-gallon 'Kimberly Queen' fern (*Nephrolepis* hybrids)
1   8-inch pot 'Florida Sweetheart' caladium (*Caladium* 'Florida Sweetheart')
1   1-quart 'Accent Coral' impatiens (*Impatiens walleriana* 'Accent Coral')
1   1-quart 'Evergold' sedge (*Carex hachijoensis* 'Evergold')

When I spotted this old cast-iron urn stored in a garage of a fellow gardener, I said, "Wow! Now there's a container with style." She replied by asking if I wanted to borrow it and I jumped at the offer. I thought it would be perfect for a wedding reception I was helping to plan. That's one of the great qualities of gardeners; they have a ready willingness to share.

I'm happy to say that this container put on quite a show for the event. It had the quality of a large cut-flower arrangement, and after the party was over, I moved it to a shady location where it retained its good looks all summer.

The large lacy fronds of the 'Kimberly' fern create a nice fan-shaped, dark green background. Both the 'Accent Coral' impatiens and the 'Florida Sweetheart' caladium seem to pop against the uniform green canvas. The lines of the fern's fronds also lead the eye right to the flowers.

The lighter coral blooms of the impatiens are at the center of the display while the darker hues of the caladiums anchor the bottom of the arrangement. Fine golden variegated blades of the 'Evergold' sedge spill informally over the sides. The plant's vertical yellow lines replicate the fluted details in the urn.

things to keep in mind

❋ In a shaded area with attention given to watering, this grouping stays colorful all summer.

❋ Occasionally pinching back the impatiens helps to keep them in bounds.

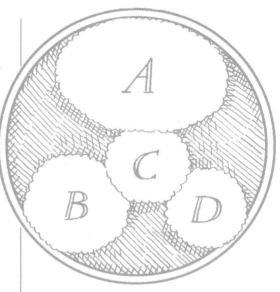

Plant List
A. *'Kimberly Queen' fern*
B. *'Florida Sweetheart' caladium*
C. *'Accent Coral' impatiens*
D. *'Evergold' sedge*

focal point

'OBOROZUKI' SWEET FLAG ACORUS

'FIREFLY LIGHT SALMON' MINI IMPATIENS

'FIREFLY IMPROVED SALMON' MINI IMPATIENS

'BRONZE BEAUTY' AJUGA

STAINED GLASSWORKS 'TRAILING ROSE' COLEUS

· No. 28 ·

SHADE • Garden Home Principle: **ENTRY**

28. Salmon Firefly Impatiens in Bronze Urn

Invite guests up the steps to your home with a matching pair of these containers on the landing at the bottom of a staircase. The effect is even more striking when the door and trim of the house are painted in a dark color with bronze accents, picking up the salmon color of the impatiens.

1 fiberglass footed urn with faux-bronze finish—
   18 inches tall × 17 inches diameter (with bowl 11 inches deep)
2 1-quart 'Firefly Improved Salmon' mini impatiens
   (*Impatiens walleriana* 'Firefly Improved Salmon')
1 1-quart 'Firefly Light Salmon' mini impatiens
   (*Impatiens walleriana* 'Firefly Light Salmon')
2 1-quart Stained Glassworks 'Trailing Rose' coleus
   (*Solenostemon scutellariodes* 'Trailing Rose')
1 1-quart 'Oborozuki' sweet flag acorus (*Acorus gramineus* 'Oborozuki')
1 1-quart 'Bronze Beauty' ajuga (*Ajuga reptans* 'Bronze Beauty')

This urn has several good selling points—besides its attractive shape and color, it is lightweight, so it's easy to move, and frostproof. Its dark color with rusty stained crevices is the perfect foil to showcase 'Firefly Salmon' and 'Light Salmon' mini impatiens. If you haven't tried these tiny impatiens, I highly recommend you get in your car and make your way to the nursery now!

An exuberant 'Trailing Rose' coleus arches up and out of the back of the urn. It seems to have an almost clairvoyant quality as it grows, filling in wherever it is needed. Its handsome maroon and pink heart-shaped leaves are a good match with the peach and pink blooms in the arrangement. The green and yellow blades of sweet flag chime in with a bright note of color.

Another element of interest in the mix of plants is the dark-colored foliage of 'Bronze Beauty' ajuga. In spring, this plant erupts in blue flowers, but its foliage alone makes it a worthy addition to this composition, softening the sharp lip of the urn as it spills seductively over the edge. Later in the season, 'Blue Moon' torenia can be substituted for the ajuga. It also has a cascading form that produces waves of blue blooms with white centers, the large bright dots creating the effect of little white moons. More than likely, this enchanting feature must have something to do with how the plant got its name.

Plant List
A. 'Firefly Improved Salmon' mini impatiens
B. 'Firefly Light Salmon' mini impatiens
C. Stained Glassworks 'Trailing Rose' coleus
D. 'Oborozuki' sweet flag acorus
E. 'Bronze Beauty' ajuga

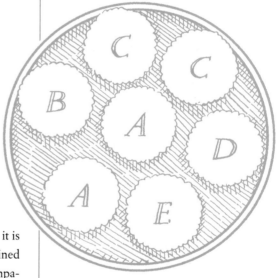

things to keep in mind
* Morning sun or filtered light encourages more blooms on the impatiens and torenia and helps to keep the coleus foliage colors bright.
* In the fall, the perennial plants, ajuga and sweet flag, can be planted in the garden.

SUN • Garden Home Principle: **ABUNDANCE**

29. Old-Fashioned Rose and Coleus Container

If you are challenged with limited garden space but love the romance of roses, this container offers a beautiful solution. When the roses take a break from blooming, the coleus and petunias are there to keep the colors coming until they return. The glazed bowl overflowing with color and fragrance is stunning when placed in a flower border that is filled with more 'Trailing Rose' coleus.

1   turquoise-glazed clay bowl—28 inches diameter × 17 inches deep

3   3-gallon 'La Marne' rose (*Rosa* 'La Marne')

3   1-gallon 'Salem' rosemary (*Rosmarinus officinalis* 'Salem')

4   1-quart Whispers 'Appleblossom' petunia (*Petunia hybrida* 'Appleblossom')

3   1-guart Stained Glassworks 'Trailing Rose' coleus (*Solenostemon scutellariodes* 'Trailing Rose')

The size and color of this container made me want to create a bold, over-the-top arrangement. This huge glazed bowl, more than two feet wide, makes an impact even in large garden spaces. Whenever you are planting a large container, it is best to fill it in its permanent location. Once it is full of soil, plants, and water, it is difficult to move.

The rose 'La Marne' is front and center in this arrangement. Here's a plant that is certainly not shy about showing off her masses of soft pink blooms. 'Trailing Rose' coleus, tucked in along the sides of the container, clamors over the sides and almost touches the ground in no time at all. Dark foliage plants like 'Trailing Rose' help create a sense of depth in the design, keeping the arrangement from looking flat or one-dimensional.

The pink centers of the coleus leaves blend in well with the pink 'Appleblossom' petunia, another great bloomer that sends out waves of color. In the center of the bowl 'Salem' rosemary gives the design some lift with its vertical spikes of gray-green foliage. While the summer progresses, the bowl itself becomes obscured from view as the plants grow and bubble over the sides.

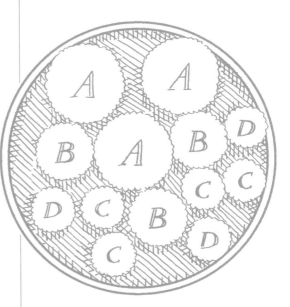

Plant List

A. *'La Marne' rose*

B. *'Salem' rosemary*

C. *Whispers 'Appleblossom' petunia*

D. *Stained Glassworks 'Trailing Rose' coleus*

things to keep in mind

❋ Protect large clay bowls from freezing temperatures. Most damage occurs when water freezes in the porous surface of the container and expands, cracking the pot.

❋ Mixing herbs and roses makes for a delightfully fragrant combination.

'LA-MARNE' ROSE

'SALEM' ROSEMARY

STAINED GLASSWORKS 'TRAILING ROSE' COLEUS

WHISPERS 'APPLEBLOSSOM' PETUNIA

• No. 29 •

SUN • Garden Home Principle: **TEXTURE, PATTERN, AND RHYTHM**

30. Peach Geraniums and Frosted Foliage

As you enjoy your morning breakfast on the deck or patio, why not do it among peach blooms and frosted foliage? This container combo looks especially smart with weathered teak patio furniture and striped cushions.

1   Europa terra-cotta container—16 inches diameter × 13 inches deep
2   1-gallon velvet centaurea (*Centaurea gymnocarpa*)
1   1-gallon 'Weeping Lavender' lantana (*Lantana montevidensis* 'Weeping Lavender')
3   3-inch pot lavender pentas (*Pentas lanceolata*)
3   1-quart 'Schoene Helena' geranium (*Pelargonium* × *hortorum* 'Schoene Helena')
2   3-inch pot 'Purple Knight' alternanthera (*Alternanthera dentata* 'Purple Knight')

Along with its soft colors and strong shapes, this arrangement has a strong sense of motion. 'Purple Knight' alternanthera and 'Schoene Helena' geraniums accomplish this effect as they push out from the container's center. Velvet centaurea joins in as it curves around to meet the lavender lantana spilling over the container's edge.

There is a comfortable "socks and shoes" feel to the blend of peach and lavender colors found in these plants. They just seem to fit together. The dark foliage of the alternanthera gives the arrangement some shadowy interest. Both the centaurea and the alternathera never slow down through the summer, the centaurea growing tall and upright while the alternanthera needles its way through the stems of the other plants.

Plant List
A. *Velvet centaurea*
B. *'Weeping Lavender' lantana*
C. *Lavender pentas*
D. *'Schoene Helena' geranium*
E. *'Purple Knight' alternanthera*

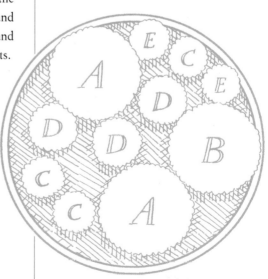

things to keep in mind

❋ This is a full-sun combination of plants. However, as the temperatures climb, the geraniums like some afternoon shade.

❋ Feed the geraniums to keep the blooms coming.

❋ Pinch back the alternanthera from time to time because it can be a vigorous grower.

SUN • Garden Home Principle: **TEXTURE, PATTERN, AND RHYTHM**

31. Vining Tepee in Raised Planter

A front porch can benefit from the addition of a tall, vertical element to help raise the eye. This tepee-shaped trellis mounted on the back of the raised planter lifts the whole arrangement to a level where it can be best appreciated. For added impact, cluster around the metal stand additional containers filled with plants from the same color family.

1   galvanized light green container—
20 inches long × 16 inches wide × 10 inches deep
1   trellis—40 inches tall (36 inches above the container)
1   metal stand—19 inches tall × 13 inches wide × 19 inches long
1   1-gallon variegated porcelain vine (*Ampelopsis brevipedunculata* 'Elegans')
1   1-gallon 'General Sikorsky' clematis (*Clematis* 'General Sikorsky')
2   1-quart variegated Cuban oregano (*Plectranthus amboinicus*)
2   1-quart 'Blue Moon' torenia (*Torenia fournieri* hybrid 'Blue Moon')
3   1-quart 'Imperial Blue' plumbago (*Plumbago auriculata* 'Imperial Blue')
1   1-quart lamb's ear (*Stachys byzantina*)
1   1-quart 'Mrs. Moon' lungwort (*Pulmonaria saccharata* 'Mrs. Moon')—
best used in partial shade settings

My Grandmother Smith planted flowers in every kind of container imaginable. Her approach was more about giving her favorite plants a good home than about being concerned with the style of the vessel. The steps to her long front porch were lined with galvanized buckets and tubs, many of which had been discarded from around her farm. With this design, I adapted her method and upgraded it a bit.

I began this project by painting the galvanized container a soft green to harmonize with the arrangement's serene blues, whites, silvers, and dark greens. Two vines are called for to ensure that the trellis is loaded with lots of foliage and bloom. 'General Sikorsky' clematis, with its impressive six-inch blue flowers, blooms off and on throughout the summer, and porcelain vine, a vigorous climber with deeply cut leaves splashed in white and pink, conspire to cover the V-shaped trellis. As an added bonus, the porcelain vine produces tiny but beautiful metallic blue berries in late summer.

The midlevel area of the tub is filled with the upright stems of 'Imperial Blue' plumbago, which has clusters of soft, blue flowers. At the base, a medley of plants including 'Blue Moon' torenia and variegated Cuban oregano mound and cascade over the edge of the tub. The soft woolly leaves of lamb's ear lend a nice texture to the composition, and 'Mrs. Moon' lungwort mixes in some interesting pattern with her silver-spotted foliage.

Plant List

A. *Variegated porcelain vine*
B. *'General Sikorsky' clematis*
C. *Variegated Cuban oregano*
D. *'Blue Moon' torenia*
E. *'Imperial Blue' plumbago*
F. *Lamb's ear*
G. *'Mrs. Moon' lungwort*

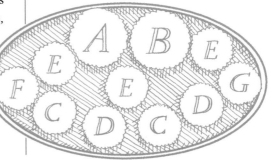

{

things to keep in mind

✳ Consider elevating containers to eye level so they can be easily viewed.

✳ Adding a trellis multiplies the levels of interest in a container.

✳ 'Mrs. Moon' lungwort does best in partial-shade settings, so if you plan to set the container in full sun,
   it would be a good idea to substitute this plant with lamb's ear.

things to keep in mind

✳ For the best performance of the flowering plants, apply fertilizer treatments regularly and avoid drought stress.

✳ The 'Salem' rosemary can be transplanted to herb or flower gardens in Zones 6 through 9.

✳ Possible plant substitutes include blue verbena, blue lantana, creeping Jenny, dusty miller, and silver licorice plant.

SUN • Garden Home Principle: **FRAMING THE VIEW**

32. Purple Profusion in a Rustic Willow Stand

This willow stand lined with sheet moss and overflowing with flowers adds a touch of rustic charm to a cottage-style home. Create a comfortable setting by situating the container arrangement alongside a pair of Adirondack chairs or some rustic twig furniture. Placed under a window, the box frames the view so the colorful blooms can be enjoyed indoors and out.

1   rustic willow stand lined with landscape fabric and sheet moss—
    34 inches long × 14 inches wide × 32 inches tall
1   1-gallon 'Salem' rosemary (*Rosmarinus officinalis* 'Salem')
2   1-quart silver Cuban oregano (*Plectranthus argentatus*)
3   1-quart 'Limelight' licorice plant (*Helichrysum petiolare* 'Limelight')
2   1-quart 'Purple Fan' fanflower (*Scaevola aemula* 'Purple Fan')
2   1-quart 'Duchess Deep Blue' torenia (*Torenia fournieri* 'Duchess Deep Blue')
2   1-quart 'Freestyle Lavender' ivy geranium (*Pelargonium peltatum* 'Freestyle Lavender')
2   1-quart 'Cascadias Improved Charlie' petunia (*Petunia hybrida* 'Cascadias Improved Charlie')
1   1-quart lamb's ear (*Stachys byzantina*)

This rustic stand has such character and appeal that I always find lots of ways to use it throughout the year. If you run across one of these, I recommend you buy it, as it has so many uses. It rarely stands empty on my front porch serving as a holder for my ever-changing seasonal displays.

Colorful gourds, pumpkins, and bittersweet can be piled in the stand for an easy fall arrangement. At the first sign of spring, fill it with containers of tulips, daffodils, and hyacinths. If you're short on time, just drop the nursery pots directly in the stand with a layer of sphagnum moss around the tops to keep the plastic containers hidden from view.

For a summer display, line the interior of the container with green sheet moss and then drape in a piece of landscape fabric before filling it with soil. The fabric holds the soil but allows the water to drain. You can use a plastic garbage bag just as well. Just remember to poke a few holes in the bottom for drainage.

The soothing palette of this arrangement calls for plants found on the color wheel's cool side: mostly blues and lavenders with a lively bit of silver and bright green thrown in. If the style of this rustic stand doesn't fit with your home's character, this sophisticated yet subtle color scheme would also suit a more elegant vessel.

Plant List
A. 'Salem' rosemary
B. Silver Cuban oregano
C. 'Limelight' licorice plant
D. 'Purple Fan' fanflower
E. 'Duchess Deep Blue' torenia
F. 'Freestyle Lavender' ivy geranium
G. 'Cascadia Improved Charlie' petunia
H. Lamb's ear

SUN • Garden Home Principle: **TIME**

33. Grandmother's Summer Sun Garden

With all the romance and charm of an old-fashioned garden, this container looks great with either a traditional- or cottage-style home. Accent your garden gate or mailbox with this living bouquet of carefree blooms.

1   gray, round fiberglass container 18 inches diameter × 16 inches deep
1   1-gallon 'Powis Castle' artemisia (*Artemisia* 'Powis Castle')
2   1-quart 'Magnus' coneflower (*Echinacea purpurea* 'Magnus')
2   1-gallon 'Ruby Star' coneflower (*Echinacea purpurea* 'Ruby Star')
2   1-quart 'Helene Von Stein' lamb's ear (*Stachys byzantina* 'Helene Von Stein')
2   1-quart 'Sentimental Blue' balloon flower (*Platycodon grandiflorus* 'Sentimental Blue')

As I began assembling this container, my goal was to capture the feel of an old-fashioned perennial garden. The combination of all the plants looked like I had dug up a corner of my grandmother's garden and transplanted it into this container. That was just the result I wanted.

   The finely cut, smoky gray leaves of 'Powis Castle' artemisia create a harmonizing effect with the cool, blue-gray fiberglass container. The artemisia serves as a tall spiky element in the back of the container while another dependable gray foliage plant, 'Helene Von Stein' lamb's ear, drapes along the front. 'Sentimental Blue' balloon flower nestles comfortably in between the lamb's ear and the pot's edge. Two varieties of coneflowers festoon the arrangement with their unique blossoms. Instead of the narrow, drooping petals displayed by their cousin, the native purple coneflower, these plants feature broad pink petals that stand erect from their orange center cones in a more horizontal manner. The arrangement is topped off with 'Magnus', Perennial Plant of the Year in 1998, and 'Ruby Star', a new strain with dark pink petals. Both are beautiful.

things to keep in mind

✻ All the plants are perennials and will bloom for several weeks at a time. Deadheading encourages more flowers.

✻ Since many perennials aren't continuous bloomers, once their flowering cycle is finished, move them into permanent locations in your garden.

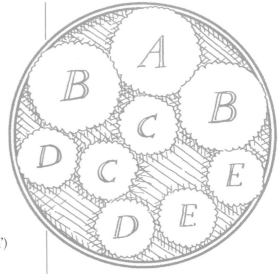

Plant List
A. *'Powis Castle' artemisia*
B. *'Ruby Star' coneflower*
C. *'Magnus' coneflower*
D. *'Helene Von Stein' lamb's ear*
E. *'Sentimental Blue' balloon flower*

'RUBY STAR' CONEFLOWER

'POWIS CASTLE' ARTEMISIA

'HELENE VON STEIN' LAMB'S EAR

'MAGNUS' CONEFLOWER

'SENTIMENTAL BLUE' BALLOON FLOWER

· No. 33 ·

whimsy

'HOOSIER HARMONY' HOSTA

'INA MAE' BEGONIA

GOLDEN CREEPING JENNY

· No. 34 ·

SHADE • Garden Home Principle: **TEXTURE, PATTERN, AND RHYTHM**

34. Begonia Shade Garden

Beguilingly simple yet quite sophisticated, this container calls for just three varieties of plants. Place several containers around the edge of a shady terrace to help define the area's boundaries, or use just one alongside a wall fountain amid a setting of garden furniture with a bronze finish.

1 round terra-cotta container painted black—18 inches diameter × 15 inches deep
1 8-inch pot 'Hoosier Harmony' hosta (*Hosta* 'Hoosier Harmony')
2 1-quart 'Ina Mae' begonia (*Begonia* × *Ina Mae*)
3 1-quart golden creeping Jenny (*Lysimachia nummularia* 'Aurea')

This shade container is an exercise in restraint, both in terms of color and the number of plants used to create the design. It is an example of how a simple combination of plants in subtle shades of green can create a complete and satisfying unit.

The large and stately 'Hoosier Harmony' hosta gives the planter an immediate sense of stature and matches the scale of the container. Its generous leaves carry undertones of the vibrant green color found in the long, flowing strands of golden creeping Jenny. Both plants create a striking contrast against the polished foliage of 'Ina Mae' begonia. The black pot echoes the shadowy begonia leaves, but the begonia is positioned in such a way as to distance it from the pot so both can be better appreciated.

While all of these plants perform well, the begonia shows its domineering side and quickly overtakes the hosta, becoming the bully in the container. But it redeems itself, for as it grows larger, its luminous pink blossoms appear and easily steal the show.

Plant List
A. *'Hoosier Harmony' hosta*
B. *'Ina Mae' begonia*
C. *Golden creeping Jenny*

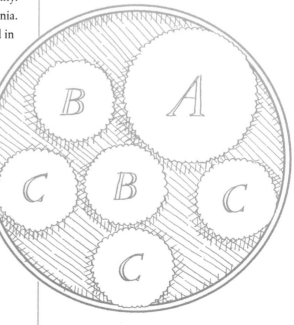

things to keep in mind

* The creeping Jenny and hosta are perennials that can be planted in the garden when the container is disassembled.
* The begonia is an annual, but cuttings can be taken and overwintered indoors to ensure that the plants will be available the following year.
* If this variety of begonia is not available, check out other members of the family that can perform with equal vigor.

SUN • Garden Home Principle: **STRUCTURE**

35. Hardy Hibiscus Garden

Is your yard covered by a deck or concrete patio with no soil in sight? Are you faced with an unsightly privacy fence or an uninspiring wall? The solution is near at hand. Assemble several of these beautiful hibiscus gardens and sprinkle them around your deck and garden to give yourself some visual relief.

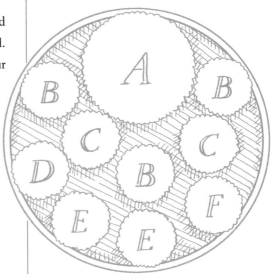

1	roll-rim terra-cotta container—19 inches diameter × 17 inches deep
1	3-gallon 'Kopper King' hibiscus (*Hibiscus moscheutos* 'Kopper King')
3	1-quart 'Black and Blue' salvia (*Salvia guaranitica* 'Black and Blue')
2	1-quart 'Oriental Limelight' artemisia (*Artemisia vulgaris* 'Oriental Limelight')
1	1-quart 'Evergold' sedge (*Carex hachijoensis* 'Evergold')
2	1-quart 'Sentimental Blue' balloon flower (*Platycodon grandiflorus* 'Sentimental Blue')
1	1-quart 'Callie Ivory II' Calibrachoa (*Calibrachoa* hybrid 'Callie Ivory II')

Plant List
A. *'Kopper King' hibiscus*
B. *'Black and Blue' salvia*
C. *'Oriental Limelight' artemisia*
D. *'Evergold' sedge*
E. *'Sentimental Blue' balloon flower*
F. *'Callie Ivory II' calibrachoa*

This container is at its prime in midsummer. That's when the 'Kopper King' hibiscus really begins to come on strong. But even before those hypnotic red-centered pink blooms open, the plant's dark purple palmate leaves bring color and visual interest to the display.

Countering the height of the hibiscus are the tall spires of 'Black and Blue' salvia, with its sky blue snapdragonlike flowers with black calyxes. The bloom of the hibiscus in combination with the salvia is sensational. 'Sentimental Blue' balloon flowers fill in the middle of the arrangement, and tickling the edge with lots of creamy blooms is 'Callie Ivory' calibrachoa, adding her own bright accent of color. The chartreuse foliage of 'Oriental Limelight' artemisia and the variegated leaves of 'Evergold' sedge help break up the mass of green foliage.

As the container fills out, its imposing height creates a strong presence in the garden. When plants become this large, it's easy to forget that they are growing out of a pot that is merely seventeen inches tall.

things to keep in mind
* These containers are ideal for people who love perennials but don't have the garden space to plant them.
* Be sure that the container gets at least six hours of sun a day.

'KOPPER KING' HIBISCUS

'ORIENTAL LIMELIGHT' ARTEMISIA

'BLACK AND BLUE' SALVIA

'EVERGOLD' SEDGE

'CALLIE IVORY II' CALIBRACHOA

'SENTIMENTAL BLUE' BALLOON FLOWER

· No. 35 ·

things to keep in mind

* Because there are numerous plants in one container, increased attention should be paid to watering and fertilization.
* Avoid using sprays that would be harmful to the hummingbirds. Remember, they feed not only on the flower nectar but also on insects.
* Find a sheltered location for the container, so the blooms stay put while the birds dine.

SUN • Garden Home Principle: **MYSTERY**

36. Hummingbird Garden

Packed with plants that hummingbirds love, this container is an irresistible lure for those tiny flying jewels. Ideal for anyone who enjoys the wonder of nature, this garden of delight should be placed in a flower border or on your deck or patio where it allows you to sit back to watch the show.

1   terra-cotta container—20 inches diameter × 16 inches deep
1   1-gallon tropical butterfly weed (*Asclepias curassavica*)
2   1-quart verbena-on-a-stick (*Verbena bonariensis*)
2   1-quart 'Salsa Rose' salvia (*Salvia splendens* 'Salsa Rose')
3   3-inch pot 'Red Butterfly' pentas (*Pentas lanceolata* 'Red Butterfly')
2   1-gallon shrimp plant (*Pachystachys lutea*)
1   1-gallon yellow bells (*Tecoma stans*)
3   1-quart 'Saratoga Lime' nicotiana (*Nicotiana* 'Saratoga Lime')
1   12-inch hanging basket, cut in half, of batface cuphea (*Cuphea llavea*)
2   1-quart 'Cascadias Improved Charlie' petunia (*Petunia hybrida* 'Cascadias Improved Charlie')

"Hummingbird magnet" was the phrase that kept running through my head as I gathered plants for this container. Watching the antics of these delightful winged acrobats buzzing in and out of my garden was so entertaining, I wanted to see if I could draw them in closer by creating a veritable candy store of flowers in a container.

Hummingbirds are especially drawn to red and orange tubular and funnel-shaped flowers. This arrangement experiments a bit by mixing the tried-and-true varieties with others to create a pot full of goodies. The resulting riot of colors and forms delights both hummingbirds and garden guests alike.

The tall wands of verbena-on-a-stick, tropical butterfly weed, and the yellow shrimp plant give height to the container. Upright and mounding plants fill in while cascading varieties soften the edges. Hot blooms of red, orange, and yellow are tempered by flowers in blue, lavender, and light green.

Hummingbirds feeding on these flowers provide hours of entertainment. It's best to plant this container in the spot where you know you will enjoy watching these tiny wonders because once filled, the pot becomes quite heavy, particularly after watering. This is a great project to share with children.

Plant List

A. *Tropical butterfly weed*
B. *Verbena-on-a-stick*
C. *'Salsa Rose' salvia*
D. *'Red Butterfly' pentas*
E. *Shrimp plant*
F. *Yellow bells*
G. *'Saratoga Lime' nicotiana*
H. *Batface cuphea*
I. *'Cascadias Improved Charlie' petunia*

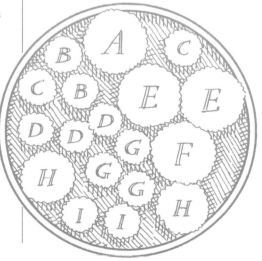

'BLACK MAGIC' ELEPHANT EAR

VELVET DUSTY MILLER

'CHAMELION' EUPHORBIA

PLECTRANTHUS

'PURPLE LADY' IRESINE

· No. 37 ·

PARTIAL SHADE • Garden Home Principle: **TEXTURE, PATTERN, AND RHYTHM**

37. Black Elephant Ears with Gray Foliage

The bold and contrasting textures in this arrangement create a dramatic focal point in a shade garden. Place the container at the entrance where you want a theatrical accent.

1	rolled-rim terra-cotta container —16 inches diameter × 16 inches deep
3	1-gallon 'Black Magic' elephant ear (*Colocasia esculenta* 'Black Magic')
2	1-gallon velvet dusty miller (*Centaurea gymnocarpa*)
1	1-quart 'Chameleon' euphorbia (*Euphorbia dulcis* 'Chameleon')
2	1-quart plectranthus (*Plectranthus fruticosus*)
2	3-inch pots purple heart (*Tradescantia pallida*)
3	3-inch pots 'Purple Lady' iresine (*Iresine herbstii* 'Purple Lady')

By chance, as I was unloading my latest plant purchases near my potting shed, I happened to place a nursery pot full of velvet dusty miller next to several large containers of 'Black Magic' elephant ears. That's all it took to convince me that they belonged together. I knew the gorgeous dark leaves of 'Black Magic' colocasia mixed well with many colors, but it was simply irresistible alongside the silvery foliage of centaurea. It was not only the color combination that urged me to make them container mates, it was also their wonderfully different leaf forms—the finely cut foliage of the dusty miller set against the large bold leaves of the 'Black Magic' was a match made in heaven.

A few smaller pots of burgundy and green foliage plants help to complete the design: 'Chameleon' euphorbia, dark-leafed purple heart, 'Purple Lady' iresine, and some plectranthus. You may recognize the plectranthus as a relative of the common houseplant Swedish ivy. Its crinkled green leaves with metallic purple undersides are beautiful cascading over the container's edge.

things to keep in mind

✳ Filtered light or morning sun and afternoon shade encourages the dark leaf colors to develop without becoming overheated and burning.

✳ Experiment with your own plant combinations to enjoy unique and personally rewarding containers of your own design.

Plant List
A. *'Black Magic' elephant ear*
B. *Velvet dusty miller*
C. *'Chamelion' euphorbia*
D. *Plectranthus*
E. *Purple heart*
F. *'Purple Lady' iresine*

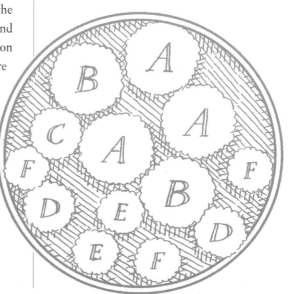

PARTIAL SHADE • Garden Home Principle: **ACCENT THE ENTRY**

38. Passion for Purple

With plants like these, the phrase "too much is just enough" would be a fitting description. This rich purple riot of blooms and foliage deserves a prominent place on your porch, patio, or deck.

2   matching slate gray terra-cotta containers—
14 inches diameter × 14 inches deep

FOR EACH CONTAINER
2   1-quart Persian shield (*Strobilanthes dyerianus*)
3   1-quart 'Accent Deep Pink' impatiens (*Impatiens walleriana* 'Accent Deep Pink')
2   1 quart 'Silver Mound' artemisia (*Artemisia schmidtiana* 'Silver Mound')
2   1-quart Whispers 'Blue Rose' petunia (*Petunia hybrida* 'Blue Rose')
1   6-pack dusty miller (*Centaurea cineraria*)

At times I feel like a mad scientist, mixing up various combinations of plants in the hopes of finding those miraculous combinations that garner jaw-dropping results. That's the level of excitement I experienced with this combination.

A volcano of color erupts from the center of the container in molten shades of purple and metallic silver, as the gorgeous foliage of Persian shield thrusts upward in a dramatic foliar display. Pink and violet blooms of the impatiens and the petunias tumble from the tips of the Persian shield's leaves all the way to the ground, seemingly in one continuous sweep, and as the "lava" moves downward, it cools, ending in a swirl of frothy gray.

Plant List
A. Persian shield
B. 'Accent Deep Pink' impatiens
C. 'Silver Mound' artemisia
D. Whispers 'Blue Rose' petunias
E. Dusty miller

things to keep in mind

⁂ Use full, mature plants to achieve this abundant look. Hanging baskets of petunias and impatiens that have long trailing stems will give you quick results.

⁂ As the summer progresses, the container benefits from afternoon shade and regular waterings.

SHADE • Garden Home Principle: **MYSTERY**

39. Tabletop Water Garden

On a hot summer day, this cool and restful container offers an oasis of comfort on a low bamboo table next to your favorite outdoor chair. For a larger, more dramatic display, position the bowl on a plinth against a tropical background of elephant ears or a banana tree.

1   green ceramic bowl—18 inches diameter × 8 inches deep
1   small water pump
1   1-quart 'Hilo Beauty' alocasia (*Alocasia* 'Hilo Beauty')
3   1-quart 'Oborozuki' sweet flag acorus (*Acorus gramineus* 'Oborozuki')
3   3-inch pot Great Blue lobelia (*Lobelia siphilitica*)

The idea that water gardens must be large and elaborate proves untrue with this compact model. A glazed ceramic bowl (without drainage holes) is easy to transform into a bubbling water bath with the help of a few water plants and a small electric water pump found in a garden center or an aquarium store. The pump is placed inside of a jar and weighed down with a stone, and then the cord is pulled over the back rim of the bowl.

Plant List
A. *'Hilo Beauty' alocasia*
B. *'Oborozuki' sweet flag acorus*
C. *Great Blue lobelia*

The planted pots are positioned to conceal the electrical cord, and the shorter pots are set on pieces of brick to display them at varying heights. A sprinkling of pebbles over the top of the potted plants keeps them from floating.

Because of the compact size of this container and the delicate bubbling and gurgling of the small pump, I place it on a table in my loggia, where I often sit and read the newspaper. The fountain provides a wonderful soothing sound and a cool serenity that is welcome on a hot summer day.

There are many wonderful varieties of water plants. Like those planted in soil, they have their preferences for certain kinds of growing conditions. These are a mix of tropical and temperate woodland plants that can coexist happily, and were selected for their ability to tolerate shade and grow in marshy conditions.

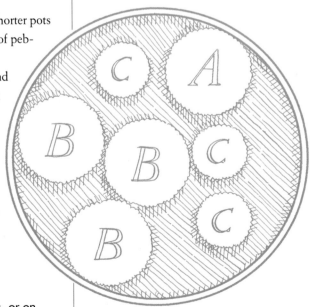

things to keep in mind

❋ Keep leaves and debris out of the water to keep it looking fresh.
❋ Small water pumps can be found at garden centers, aquarium stores, or on the Internet.

GREAT BLUE LOBELIA

'HILO BEAUTY' ALOCASIA

'OBOROZUKI' SWEET FLAG ACORUS

· No. 39 ·

MEXICAN HEATHER

'LITTLE WHITE PET' ROSE

'KEWENSIS' TRAILING EUONYMUS

· No. 40 ·

SUN • Garden Home Principle: **ENCLOSURE**

40. Patio Rose Summer Bouquet

Little White Pet is one of many varieties of roses well suited for containers. Fill several planters with this easy combination and space them evenly along the edge of a deck or terrace to beautify the setting throughout the summer and well into fall.

1	wooden whiskey half-barrel—22 inches diameter × 16 inches deep
2	3-gallon 'Little White Pet' rose
6	4-inch pots Mexican heather (*Cuphea hyssopifolia*)
8	4-inch pots 'Kewensis' trailing euonymus (*Euonymus fortunei* 'Kewensis')

Like racehorses and champion dogs, roses have pedigrees, too. It's fun to learn about the lineage of these plants because many have fascinating histories. For instance, 'Little White Pet' is a dwarf offshoot of its full-sized parent 'Felicite et Perpétue'. That great ancestor is an old-fashioned rambling rose whose garden debut dates to 1827. The rose blooms magnificently, but only once in the spring. Happily for us, 'Little White Pet' didn't inherit that single flowering trait; it is rarely without full white pompom blossoms. Unlike its full-sized forebearer, 'Little White Pet' stays compact in size (under two feet), which makes it the perfect choice for small gardens and container plantings. As you explore the world of roses, you will discover that some require more care than others. This little rose scores again in its disease-resistant nature, so little maintenance is needed to keep it looking its best.

Planting this sweet little rose in a rugged wooden barrel creates a surprising contrast. Mexican heather adds its glossy green leaves and scores of tiny lavender blooms give the arrangement a lift. To help soften the hard edge of the barrel, 'Kewensis' trailing euonymous (also known as dwarf wintercreeper) tumbles over the sides.

things to keep in mind
* This rose requires regular feeding to keep the blooms coming.
* Remove spent blossoms to encourage more flower buds.

Plant List
A. *'Little White Pet' rose*
B. *Mexican heather*
C. *'Kewensis' trailing euonymus*

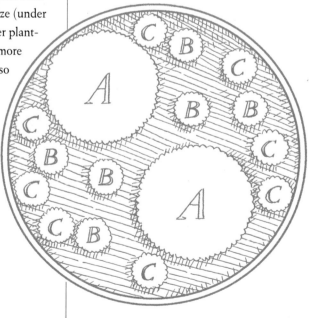

AuTUMN

When apples and pumpkins appear at the local road-
side stands and farmers' markets, I'm ready for a change
in seasons. At last, the relentless heat of summer lifts,
taking with it the air's heavy haze and leaving behind
a blissfully clear, forever-blue sky. With the daylight
hours dwindling and autumn's first frost just around the
corner, it's time to throw caution to the wind and
pour on the color in my garden and container designs.

I LOVE TO CREATE BIG SHOCKS OF COLOR IN MY CONTAINERS TO MATCH THE SPIRIT OF AUTUMN: FIERY RED, ACID GREEN, AND BOLD ORANGE COLLIDE WITH LAVENDER, PINK, AND DEEP GOLD. I ALSO LIKE TO MIX IN DARK-LEAF PLANTS LIKE SWEET POTATO VINE 'BLACKIE', PURPLE CABBAGE, AND BLOODY SORREL. THESE DEEPLY SATURATED FOLIAGE PLANTS HELP GROUND THE FIRE BURST OF COLORS THAT ALL TOO SOON WILL BECOME FADING EMBERS.

There's a now-or-never feel to this season, with no time to wait for plants to grow into something memorable, so I buy only mature plants for my containers. I also like to stack up piles of pumpkins and gourds combined with stalks of corn and dried flowers next to my containers in order to create an ensemble of objects.

Autumn is the time to take one last look at my summer arrangements and decide which plants stay and which ones go. Many summer flowers remain vibrant and colorful throughout the fall, while others are ready to give up the ghost and make their final contribution in the compost pile. I find many of the planters just need a little lift, so I remove the spent plants and slip in robust pots of mums, peppers, pansies, and ornamental grasses.

Pour on the autumn color with this window box planted in a sassy medley of purple Mexican salvia, gold lantana, dinosaur kale, golden creeping Jenny, red ornamental peppers, and a bonanza of bronze chrysanthemums.

If there are any perennials in the summer containers that I want to use again, I transplant them into my flowerbeds and give them a chance to settle in before cold temperatures arrive—although I must admit that I'm often guilty of procrastinating with this task. Every fall I seem to convince myself that the first frost will be unusually late, and I can enjoy a few more blissful weeks of autumn before the final curtain comes down.

SLIP-IN • Garden Home Principle: **COLOR**

41. Big, Bold Autumn Color

Versatile in use, this container can stand alone as a focal point in a garden room or, for even more impact, it can be grouped with two other containers. To create an ensemble, fill one of its companion pots with more purple cabbage and the other with 'Debonair' chrysanthemums.

1   roll-rim terra-cotta container—21 inches diameter × 14 inches deep

6   4-inch pots 'Debonair' chrysanthemum
(*Chrysanthemum* × *morifolium* 'Debonair')

1   1-gallon bloody sorrel (*Rumex sanguineus*)

2   6-packs purple cabbage (*Brassica oleracea*)

2   6-packs 'Velour Blue Bronze' viola (*Viola* × *wittrockiana* 'Velour Blue Bronze')

1   1-quart Stained Glassworks 'Trailing Rose' coleus (*Solenostemon scutellariodes*) 'Trailing Rose'

2   1-gallon 'Red Sensation' cordyline (*Cordyline australis* 'Red Sensation')

I'm one of those people who just can't throw anything away. I seem to be in the use-and-reuse mode whether I'm redecorating the house or making changes to the garden. This container is an example of how I restyled a summer arrangement to give it more of an autumnal feel.

During the summer, a pot of geraniums, torenia, and petunias flourished in a medley of purple and pink. In the fall, they were removed and replaced with new plants to usher in a slightly deeper palette of autumnal colors in burgundy, pink, and purple. Cabbage is an often overlooked jewel for fall gardens and containers. Its broad leaves and deep color add a nice accent to this arrangement.

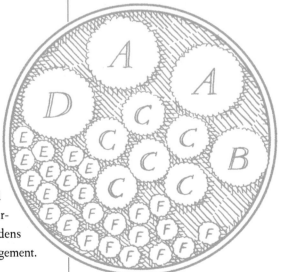

things to keep in mind

✳ Use a hand trowel to gently remove the summer plants. You may need to cut through established roots enmeshed in the soil.

✳ Dig holes for the new plants that allow you to match soil lines. Fill in the gaps around each plant with soil and tamp to fill in air pockets.

✳ Once all the new plants are in place, water the container thoroughly.

Plant List

A. *'Red Sensation' cordyline*

B. *Stained Glassworks 'Trailing Rose' coleus*

C. *'Debonair' chrysanthemum*

D. *Bloody sorrel*

E. *Purple cabbage*

F. *'Velour Blue Bronze' viola*

'RED SENSATION' CORDYLINE

'VELOUR BLUE BRONZE' VIOLA

'DEBONAIR' CHRYSANTHEMUM

BLOODY SORREL

PURPLE CABBAGE

STAINED GLASSWORKS 'TRAILING ROSE' COLEUS

No. 41

SUN • Garden Home Principle: **ENCLOSURE**

42. 'Sweet Autumn' Clematis Combo

A garden becomes more beautiful with vines, particularly when they are those of 'Sweet Autumn' clematis. Adding a trellis to a container gives you a chance to soften vertical surfaces with this fall-blooming beauty. Place the box against a sunny blank wall or create some privacy by spacing a series of these trellised boxes around the perimeter of a garden room.

1   plastic Earth Box—33 inches long × 15 inches wide × 12 inches deep
1   framed wood box—39 inches long × 15 inches wide × 13 inches deep
1   painted wooden trellis—36 inches wide × 32 inches above container
1   2-gallon 'Sweet Autumn' clematis (*Clematis paniculata* 'Sweet Autumn')
2   2-gallon 'Yellow Nicole' chrysanthemum (*Chrysanthemum* × *morifolium* 'Yellow Nicole')
1   1-gallon 'Purple Moon' torenia (*Torenia fournieri* hybrid 'Purple Moon')
2   1-quart 'Purple Moon' torenia (*Torenia fournieri* hybrid 'Purple Moon')
4   1-quart 'Black and Blue' salvia (*Salvia guaranitica* 'Black and Blue')

Plant List
A. *'Sweet Autumn' clematis*
B. *'Yellow Nicole' chrysanthemum*
C. *'Purple Moon' torenia*
D. *'Black and Blue' salvia*

While attending an American Horticultural Society meeting, I heard about a new kind of planter called the Earth Box. It was a special type of plastic container designed with a unique growing system that automatically feeds and waters your plants. I was intrigued, so I decided to try one in my garden.

I treated it as a plastic liner and housed it in a wooden planter with an attached trellis along the back. To match the garden's décor, I painted the box and trellis a sky-stealing shade of blue. Although the Earth Box was developed primarily for small-scale vegetable gardens, I used it to grow a variety of ornamental plants.

Bright 'Yellow Nicole' chrysanthemums are beautiful accents against the container's chalky blue color. 'Purple Moon' torenias play among the mum's button-shaped blooms and trail down the front of the container. The back of the planter is filled with spikes of 'Black and Blue' salvia. The tracery of vines ascending the trellis belongs to 'Sweet Autumn' clematis. While other members of the clematis family show their colors earlier in the season, this plant waits until the fall to put on its glorious show. Once the performance starts, the vine is covered with thousands of tiny white starlike flowers that sweetly perfume the air. Now that's entertainment!

things to keep in mind
* Deadhead the spent chrysanthemum blooms to keep it looking fresh.
* Mums can dry out quickly, so water and feed the plants regularly.
* Bees are attracted to the clematis blooms, so place the container in a spot where they won't bother your activities.

PARTIAL SHADE • Garden Home Principle: **FOCAL POINT**

43. Jack Frost Shade Basket

For a fall gathering, display this basket as a tabletop centerpiece or use it to welcome your guests as an accent by the front door. Devotees of monochromatic color schemes will find this white-on-white display to be elegantly simple but striking. It may also be the perfect planter for an autumn wedding or a silver anniversary party.

1	moss-lined open-weave iron basket—21 inches diameter × 10 inches deep
1	bag of sphagnum moss (presoaked)
1	8- to 10-inch hanging basket 'Sonic White' New Guinea impatiens (*Impatiens × hybrida* 'Sonic White')
3	1-gallon 'Stephanie' Prophet Series chrysanthemum (*Chrysanthemum × morifolium* 'Stephanie')
2	1-quart variegated flax lily (*Dianella tasmanica* 'Variegata')

All it takes to make this beautiful display is the combination of three plants and just a few minutes to assemble it. In fact, if you are running short of time, you don't even need to remove the plants from their nursery pots. Simply line the wire basket with moss and set the plants inside, making a few minor adjustments to elevate each container by sticking empty nursery pots of varying sizes below them. Cover the tops of the pots with more moss. Once that process is done, so are you.

The trick to creating an effective monochromatic design is selecting plants that offer a contrast in their shapes, forms, and patterns. This allows an arrangement to sing by virtue of its differences. In this display, the striped foliage of the variegated flax lily sets off the mum's large white blooms as well as the round blossoms of the 'Sonic White' New Guinea impatiens. The flax offers some separation between the two flowering plants, enabling both to be better appreciated.

things to keep in mind

* Presoak the nursery pots before positioning them in the container.
* When the soil is dry to the touch, it's time to water.
* Protect a solid surface beneath a container with a saucer to collect the water.

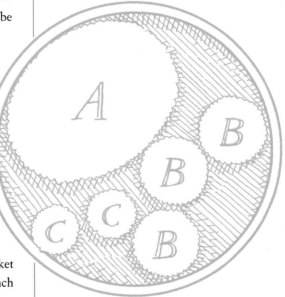

Plant List
A. *'Sonic White' New Guinea impatiens*
B. *'Stephanie' Prophet Series chrysanthemum*
C. *Variegated flax lily*

'SONIC WHITE' NEW GUINEA IMPATIENS

'STEPHANIE' PROPHET SERIES CHRYSANTHEMUM

VARIEGATED FLAX LILY

· No. 48 ·

SUN • Garden Home Principle: **STRUCTURE**

44. Fall Garden Ensemble

Trumpet the beginning of the fall harvest with this lively collection of autumn plants and pumpkins. Placed between two windows on a patio or deck, this tall jardinière fills in those narrow blank spaces with color and bloom. Its tall vertical element also makes a striking appointment near an entry.

1   round mustard-color ceramic container topped in white glaze—
    21 inches diameter × 25 inches deep
1   wood bushel basket—18 inches diameter × 12 inches deep

IN CERAMIC CONTAINER

2   1-gallon purple fountain grass (*Pennisetum setaceum* 'Rubrum')
2   1-gallon 'Grace' Prophet Series chrysanthemum
    (*Chrysanthemum × morifolium* 'Grace')
3   1-quart 'Lady in Red' salvia (*Salvia coccinea* 'Lady in Red')
1   1-gallon 'Fireworks' goldenrod (*Solidago rugosa* 'Fireworks')
2   1-quart dinosaur kale (*Brassica oleracea* 'Lacinato')
2   1-quart 'Red Missile' ornamental pepper (*Capsicum annuum* 'Red Missile')
1   1-gallon batface cuphea (*Cuphea llavea*)
2   1-quart purple heart (*Tradescantia pallida*)
1   1-gallon eyeball plant (*Spilanthes acmella*)

IN BUSHEL BASKET

3   1-gallon 'Sunny Linda' Prophet Series chrysanthemum
    (*Chrysanthemum × morifolium* 'Sunny Linda')

When fall rolls around, I find myself in the mood for an entirely different color palette. When I spied this tall mustard-colored glazed jar, it seemed to be the perfect holder for a harvest-themed display. Since the container was so tall, I wanted to anchor the design with a plant of equal stature that would counterbalance its height. Tall purple fountain grass filled the order nicely with its burgundy foliage and pendulous red-tinged foxtail flowers.

This arrangement has the feel of an abundant harvest. 'Grace' chrysanthemum is a standout, and 'Fireworks' goldenrod gives the display a burst of energy with its yellow blooms rocketing up and out of the container. The aptly named dinosaur kale adds textural fun. For more autumnal sparks, 'Lady in Red' salvia joins in with its spiky red blooms along with the 'Red Missile' ornamental pepper.

Plant List

A. *Purple fountain grass*
B. *'Grace' Prophet Series chrysanthemum*
C. *'Lady in Red' salvia*
D. *'Fireworks' goldenrod*
E. *Dinosaur kale*
F. *'Red Missile' ornamental pepper*
G. *Batface cuphea*
H. *Purple heart*
I. *Eyeball plant*
J. *'Sunny Linda' Prophet Series chrysanthemum*

things to keep in mind

❋ Add pumpkins and gourds with planted containers to make a seasonal ensemble.

❋ Keep chrysanthemums well watered. They tend to wilt quickly.

❋ Counterbalance a tall container with tall plants.

texture

SUN • Garden Home Principle: **COLOR**

45. Coleus and Burgundy Mum Combination

The deeper colors of the fall season are well displayed in this pleasing combination of plants. Show it off next to your mailbox or display it as a feature on your patio or deck. Autumn is an ideal time to be bold with color.

1 terra-cotta container—17 inches diameter × 14 inches deep
2 1-gallon 'Chocolate' white snakeroot (*Eupatorium rugosum* 'Chocolate')
1 1-gallon 'Red Sensation' cordyline (*Cordyline australis* 'Red Sensation')
1 1-quart Stained Glassworks 'Kiwi Fern' Coleus (*Solenostemon scutellarioides* 'Kiwi Fern')
2 1-quart 'San Takao' autumn sage (*Salvia gregii* 'San Takao')
1 4-inch pot 'Blackie' sweet potato vine (*Ipomoea batatas* 'Blackie')
1 1-gallon 'Beth' Prophet Series chrysanthemum (*Chrysanthemum × moriflorium* 'Beth')
1 1-gallon 'Barbara' Prophet Series chrysanthemum (*Chrysanthemum × moriflorium* 'Barbara')

Plants that had been growing in spring and summer containers are ideal ingredients for fashioning new autumn displays. In this design, several colorful foliage plants provide a backdrop for the star performers: 'Beth' and 'Barbara' chrysanthemums. 'Beth' has large, dark purple blooms and 'Barbara' displays lighter-hued pompom blossoms. They are encircled with deep burgundy foliage from the trailing sweet potato vine, the spiked blades of 'Red Sensation' cordyline, and the burgundy, pink, and yellow leaves of 'Kiwi Fern' coleus. Combining these summer standouts with the mums creates a complete and satisfying display.

Two small 'San Takao' autumn sage plants, with spikes of peachy pink flowers, and 'Chocolate' snakeroot, with its chocolate foliage, red stems, and clusters of white flowers, add the finishing touch. The snakeroot plant's name sounds menacing, but it's actually not. The plant prefers lots of moisture and afternoon shade, so this arrangement doesn't match its ideal conditions. However, autumn's cooler temperatures enable it to tolerate a full-sun location with its sun-loving companions.

Plant List
A. *'Chocolate' white snakeroot*
B. *'Red Sensation' cordyline*
C. *Stained Glassworks 'Kiwi Fern' coleus*
D. *'San Takao' autumn sage*
E. *'Blackie' sweet potato vine*
F. *'Beth' Prophet Series chrysanthemum*
G. *'Barbara' Prophet Series chrysanthemum*

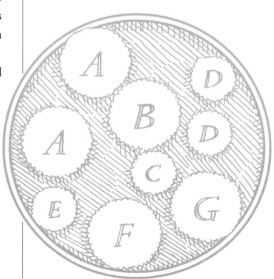

things to keep in mind

❋ Plant the container in late summer when mums are ready to bloom.
❋ Select mums that are heavily budded for longer flowering time.
❋ Terra cotta containers need winter protection in cold climates.

SHADE • Garden Home Principle: **TEXTURE, PATTERN, AND RHYTHM**

46. Shade Arrangement in a Footed Urn

Rich foliage and subtle blooms make this an elegant accent for the shade garden. It's the perfect foil to the season's riotous colors.

1   fiberglass footed urn with faux-bronze finish—
    18 inches tall × 17 inches diameter (with bowl 11 inches deep)
2   1-gallon 'Tojen' toad lily (*Tricyrtis hirta* 'Tojen')
2   4-inch pots autumn fern (*Dryopteris erythrosora*)
1   1-gallon 'Purple Moon' torenia (*Torenia fournieri* hybrid 'Purple Moon')
2   1-quart 'Bunny Blue' sedge (*Carex laxiculmis* 'Bunny Blue')
2   1-quart 'Brandywine' foam flower (*Tiarella cordifolia* 'Brandywine')

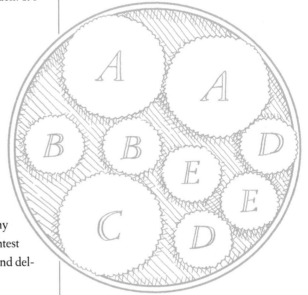

It's always fun to see which containers get the most attention from visitors to my garden. Surprisingly, it isn't always the one with the biggest flowers or the brightest colors. For instance, this container with its subtle shades, interesting foliage, and delicate blooms causes many people to stop and take a closer look.

The tall, airy 'Tojen' toad lily is one of my favorite fall plants. Its leaves alternate on two sides of its upright stems, and in late summer, when many flowering plants are waning, it displays beautiful lavender and white blooms that look like tiny orchids. The torrent of 'Purple Moon' torenia spilling out of the front of the urn also draws a lot of attention. The dark blue blossoms on this plant appear and reappear for weeks from early summer to frost. 'Bunny Blue' sedge softens the container's outer edge with its blue-green blades. The 'Brandywine' foam flower's maple-shaped leaves take on a lovely bronze hue in the fall. Additional color comes from the autumn fern, a hardy evergreen plant that thrives in Zones 5 to 9. As temperatures fall, its deep glossy green fronds revert to copper tones.

Plant List
A. 'Tojen' toad lily
B. Autumn fern
C. 'Purple Moon' torenia
D. 'Bunny Blue' sedge
E. 'Brandywine' foam flower

things to keep in mind

* The leaf edges of toad lilies have a tendency to turn brown under stress. To keep it happy and vigorous, make sure the plant is well watered and in a shady location.
* The fern is also intolerant of drought conditions.
* Aside from the torenia, all of these plants are perennials that could be planted in a shade garden before the ground freezes.

'TOJEN' TOAD LILY

AUTUMN FERN

'BUNNY BLUE' SEDGE

'PURPLE MOON' TORENIA

'BRANDYWINE' FOAM FLOWER

· No. 46 ·

things to keep in mind

* The mums are perennial and can be planted outdoors in Zones 4 to 9, and the dianthus can later be added to a bed of winter annuals.

* This container maintains its good looks for a long period of time. The 'Debonair' mums are early-fall bloomers; when they are through flowering, the dianthus continues to bloom and the foliage plants remain vibrant until frost.

* The beschoneria should be lifted from the container and placed in a protected area to overwinter in climates that experience freezing temperatures.

SUN • Garden Home Principle: **SHAPE AND FORM**

47. Classic Urn with Trailing Coleus

This container is so versatile that it can be used quite successfully in many settings. Alone, it serves beautifully as a focal point in a garden room. A pair accenting an entryway or path to a front door would also be appealing and a series of planters spaced evenly across the edge of a formal terrace to create a sense of rhythmic punctuation would be even more stunning.

1   black metal urn—29 inches tall × 22 inches diameter
     (with 17-inch inside diameter)
1   1-gallon curly yucca (*Beschorneria tubiflora*)
8   3-inch pot 'Debonair' chrysanthemum
     (*Chrysanthemum × morifolium* 'Debonair')
6   3-inch pot annual pink dianthus (*Dianthus chinensis*)
3   3-inch pots 'Silver Mist' licorice plant (*Helichrysum petiolatum* 'Silver Mist')
2   1-quart Stained Glassworks 'Trailing Rose' coleus
     (*Solenostemon scutellarioides* 'Trailing Rose')
8   plugs from 2 6-packs dusty miller (*Centaurea cineraria*)

This container design began with my desire to showcase an unusual plant for which I have a weakness. Beschorneria is a Mexican native that is related to the more well known agave. I could not resist carrying two of these back with me on an airplane after spotting them at a friend's nursery on Long Island. It was those coiled straplike leaves that got to me. They looked like they had been styled with a curling iron.

There are several different species of beschorneria and most of them are not frost tolerant. In the spring they may feature striking, brightly colored flower spikes that are three to five feet tall, but this inconsistent flowering is not usually why it is grown. This plant is really all about its shape and form. Its growth habit projects a feeling of graceful motion, which is echoed in this design with delicate vines and the urn's curves and flares.

Small containers of soft pink 'Debonair' chrysanthemums and dark pink dianthus act as upright cushions of color throughout the urn. Small plugs of dusty miller are integrated easily among the other plants, adding downy silver accents. The upright, arching shape and burgundy and pink foliage of the 'Trailing Rose' coleus enhance the pink-flowering plants as it weaves through the mums before cascading over the urn's edge. The petite silver leaves of the 'Silver Mist' licorice plants also spill over the lip, mimicking the spirals of the beschorneria and the curves of the coleus while displaying its affinity for the dusty miller by repeating the soft gray of its leaves.

Plant List
A. *Curly yucca*
B. *'Debonair' chrysanthemum*
C. *Annual pink dianthus*
D. *'Silver Mist' licorice plant*
E. *Stained Glassworks 'Trailing Rose' coleus*
F. *Dusty miller*

SUN • Garden Home Principle: **WHIMSY**

48. Cool Autumn Sun Container

For a delightful surprise, use these containers as decorative accents in your vegetable garden, a more utilitarian area of the garden that is often overlooked when it comes to ornamental touches. The cabbage used in the arrangement helps the planter fit right in with other cool seasonal vegetables you may be growing at that time.

1   round terra-cotta container—18 inches diameter × 16 inches deep
2   1-gallon velvet centaurea (*Centaurea gymnocarpa*)
1   1-gallon 'Hameln' dwarf fountain grass (*Pennisetum alopecuroides* 'Hameln')
2   1-gallon white button-type chrysanthemum (*Chrysanthemum × morifolium*)
1   1-gallon 'Penny Citrus Mix' viola (*Viola cornuta* 'Penny Citrus Mix')
2   3-inch pots 'Variegated Mint Rose' scented geranium
      (*Pelargonium graveolens* 'Variegated Mint Rose')
12   plugs from 2 6-packs cabbage (*Brassica oleracea*)

This arrangement is designed to create a little pocket of serenity. Gray- and silver-foliage plants have a way of evoking a calm and tranquil feeling. The design begins with 'Hameln' fountain grass, planted in the back. The plant provides height, first with its wispy blades of foliage and later, as the plant matures, with its fuzzy cream-colored seed heads. Filling in the center, as a filigreed backdrop to the more solid leaves and flowers, is the velvet centaurea. Soothing with its similarity, its frosty gray foliage blends with the blue-gray cabbage leaves and the white button-shaped mums. To keep the peace but not at the cost of unsettling the balance, a few bits of bright color are mixed in. A gentle array of gold, yellow, and white blooms from the 'Penny Citrus Mix' violas bring a soft glow to the composition and echo the yellow florets found at the center of the mums' white blossoms. The yellow tint in the leaves of the 'Variegated Mint Rose' scented geranium makes the unity between these plants complete.

things to keep in mind

❋ Water the container daily to accommodate the needs of the large competing plants.
❋ Feed the container to encourage lots of viola blossoms.
❋ At the end of the growing season the perennials can be planted outside. Garden mums are hardy in Zones 4 to 9 and the fountain grass is hardy in Zones 5 to 9. The violas can be planted in winter annual beds and the cabbages can be planted there or in the vegetable garden. The scented geranium can be brought indoors to grow on a sunny windowsill.

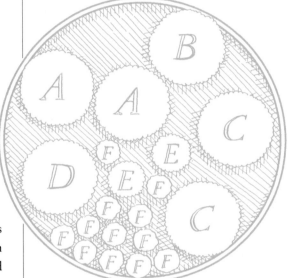

Plant List
A. *Velvet centaurea*
B. *'Hameln' dwarf fountain glass*
C. *White Button-type chrysanthemum*
D. *'Penny Citrus Mix' viola*
E. *'Variegated Mint Rose' scented geranium*
F. *Cabbage*

'VARIEGATED MINT ROSE' SCENTED GERANIUM

VELVET CENTAUREA

'HAMELN' DWARF FOUNTAIN GLASS

CABBAGE

'PENNY CITRUS MIX' VIOLA

WHITE BUTTON-TYPE CHRYSANTHEMUM

· No. 48 ·

accent the entry

SUN • Garden Home Principle: **TEXTURE, PATTERN, AND RHYTHM**

49. Shades of Rose, Pink, and Blue

This collection of soft, blushing colors is sure to inspire you to create several containers using this design. Place the boxes along the edge of a deck or patio to create a sense of rhythm and visual interest.

1   gray fiberglass window box—26 inches long × 12 inches wide × 12 inches deep
3   1-quart 'Sparkling Burgundy' pineapple lily (*Eucomis comosa* 'Sparkling Burgundy')
3   6-inch pots 'Felicia' chrysanthemum (*Chrysanthemum × morifolium* 'Felicia')
4   1-quart dinosaur kale (*Brassica oleracea* 'Lacinato')
2   1-quart Stained Glassworks 'Trailing Rose' coleus (*Solenostemon scutellarioides* 'Trailing Rose')
3   1-quart 'Glacier' English ivy (*Hedera helix* 'Glacier')
3   6-packs 'Penny Lane' mix viola (*Viola hybrida* 'Penny Lane')

Travel certainly has a way of broadening one's view of the world. It's an opportunity to gather fresh ideas and discover new plants along the way. After a trip to Holland several years ago, I saw some beautiful containers using pineapple lilies, and I returned home with the desire to try them in some of my designs. They looked so exotic that I thought they would be a fun addition to my garden.

'Sparkling Burgundy' pineapple lily clamored for inclusion in several of my container plantings from early spring right through fall. In this design, 'Sparkling Burgundy' pineapple lily's broad, shiny, wine-red leaves preside over an assembly of pink, blue-gray, and burgundy. 'Felicia' chrysanthemum, usually one of the earliest blooming mums, adds its pink-petaled, yellow-centered daisylike blooms to the mix. In this composition, the glaucous-leaved dinosaur kale, a nutritious heirloom vegetable with reptilelike foliage, is included for its ornamental value. While they can get quite large, four small-sized plants are the right scale to nestle in next to the early-blooming mums. The 'Trailing Rose' coleus flatters the pink mums with its fluid stems of burgundy and pink foliage while echoing the pineapple lily leaves.

Plugs of 'Penny Lane' mix violas are tucked in the front edges, introducing blues and purples to the mix. The steel gray-green 'Glacier' ivy tumbling down the front of the container harmonizes with the pink blooms, the blue-tinged foliage, and the soft gray container.

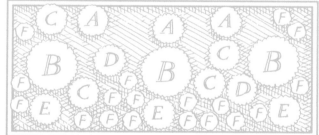

Plant List
A. 'Sparkling Burgundy' pineapple lily
B. 'Felicia' chrysanthemum
C. Dinosaur kale
D. Stained Glassworks 'Trailing Rose' coleus
E. 'Glacier' English ivy
F. 'Penny Lane' mix violas

things to keep in mind

✳ The fiberglass container can remain outside during the cold months without becoming damaged.
✳ The flowers may continue to perform in areas with mild winters.

SUN • Garden Home Principle: **SHAPE AND FORM**

50. White Mums and Variegated Foliage

All-white autumn container gardens are particularly striking when displayed on porches, decks, and patios if white is the dominant color of a home's trim or fences. The monochromatic arrangement maintains interest by combining plants with contrasting shapes and forms to create a sophisticated look.

1   terra-cotta container—20 inches diameter × 11 inches deep
1   2-gallon 'Variegatus' Japanese silver grass (*Miscanthus sinensis* 'Variegatus')
4   1-quart variegated flax lily (*Dianella tasmanica* 'Variegata')
2   8-inch pots 'Tolima' chrysanthemum (*Chrysanthemum* × *morifolium* 'Tolima')
2   1-gallon English ivy (*Hedera helix*)

Over the years I've come to rely on the timeless beauty of terra-cotta pots as the versatile container material that goes with any gardening style. They are just a natural fit in the garden. While the ubiquitous rimmed pot, called a chime rim, is the form that we most often see at garden centers, terra-cotta containers can be found in many other shapes. This arrangement features a pot with a narrow base that flares into a vase shape at the top. This shape seems to complement the bouquetlike quality of this arrangement. My rule of thumb about containers is that the pot should show off the plants, not the other way around.

This arrangement follows my Three-Shape Rule of combining three complementary plant forms: tall and spiky, round and full, and trailing or cascading. Variegated silver grass serves as the tall and spiky element. The brightening effect of its green-and-white-striped leaves harmonizes nicely with the monochromatic color scheme. The green-and-white-striped blades of the variegated flax lilies add another spiky element. The round and full form of the 'Tolima' chrysanthemum, whose blanket of white blossoms gives the appearance of an early snowfall, fills in the middle of the container. A skirt of green English ivy trailing down the container's front and sides completes the look.

Plant List
A. *'Variegatus' Japanese silver grass*
B. *Variegated flax lily*
C. *'Tolima' chrysanthemum*
D. *English ivy*

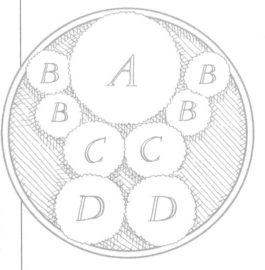

things to keep in mind

❋ The green ivy could be substituted with a white variegated ivy or variegated Cuban oregano.

❋ In hotter climates, the ivy and variegated flax lily might appreciate afternoon shade.

❋ Perennials that can be transplanted to the garden include the English ivy (Zones 5 to 10), Japanese silver grass (Zones 6 to 9), garden mums (Zones 4 to 9), and variegated flax lily (Zones 8b to 10).

'VARIEGATUS' JAPANESE SILVER GRASS

VARIEGATED FLAX LILY

'TOLIMA' CHRYSANTHEMUM

ENGLISH IVY

· No. 50 ·

SUN • Garden Home Principle: **FOCAL POINT**

51. Shades of Autumn Flower Box

These nearly square containers can stand alone or can be mixed in with other members of an ensemble. Try combining them with other contrasting container forms, such as a low dish or a vase. Square containers fit neatly next to a mailbox, nestled alongside the supporting post, which would be a perfect spot for this design.

1 terra-cotta window box—17 inches long × 9 inches wide × 15 inches deep
1 1-gallon 'Foxy Natasha' European Prophet Series chrysanthemum (*Chrysanthemum* × *morifolium* 'Foxy Natasha')
1 1-gallon copper plant (*Acalypha godseffiana* 'Heterophylla')
1 1-gallon bloody sorrel (*Rumex sanguineus*)
1 5-inch pot 'Tricolor' sage (*Salvia officinalis* 'Tricolor')
1 10- to 12-inch hanging basket, cut in half, of 'Purple and Gold' Luminaire Series trailing snapdragon (*Antirrhinum majus* 'Purple and Gold')
2 1-quart yellow gerbera daisies (*Gerbera jamesonii*)

To make it easy on yourself, go for a design that doesn't take much time but delivers an immediate, heavy visual impact. This unusually shaped terra-cotta window box caught my eye with its tall vertical lines in relation to its overall compact size. Sometimes it's the proportions alone that create something distinctive or different.

Here, a large pot of 'Foxy Natasha' chrysanthemums creates an instant autumnal bouquet. This prolific early-flowering variety has dark red ray petals and a bright yellow daisy eye. Yellow gerbera daisies in front of the mums act as the bright focal point in the arrangement. The 'Purple and Gold' trailing snapdragons dance along the front of the container, the blooms in varying shades of red echoing the mums and the sparks of yellow picking up the tones of the gerbera daisies.

Three foliage plants are tucked in for added interest. On one side 'Tricolor' sage, a variegated form of the common herb with leaves of gray-green, cream, and touches of pink add a festive touch. Bloody sorrel, a vigorous perennial with dark green, tongue-shaped leaves threaded with blood-red veins, balances the other side of the container. The third foliage plant is a variety of a subtropical copper plant. It is a dwarf variety called 'Heterophylla' that has thin multicolored leaves that intensify in color with exposure to the sun. Its bushy growth habit makes it a good filler plant in a container.

Plant List
A. *'Foxy Natasha' European Prophet Series chrysanthemum*
B. *Copper plant*
C. *Bloody sorrel*
D. *'Tricolor' sage*
E. *'Purple and Gold' Luminaire Series trailing snapdragon*
F. *Yellow gerbera daisies*

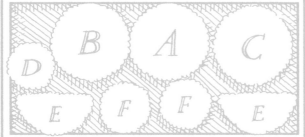

things to keep in mind

* As temperatures fall, the terra-cotta window box should be protected from freezing weather.
* Perennials that can be transplanted to the garden include 'Tricolor' salvia (Zones 6 to 9), bloody sorrel (Zones 4 to 8), and garden mums (Zones 4 to 9).
* Shelter the copper plant indoors during cooler months as a houseplant on a sunny windowsill (hardy only in Zone 10 or higher).

WiNTER

It is during the cold months that my garden reveals some of its more subtle beauty in the form of unusual barks, colorful berries, winter blooms, and evergreen foliage. When designing a four-season garden, I always make sure to include plants with these qualities to help brighten the winter landscape. The same holds true for my container designs. Gone are the bright colors of the growing season, but there are still many ways to add interest to winter pots.

EXPECTATIONS FOR GARDENS ARE LOWER IN WINTER, SO I FEEL I HAVE GREATER LICENSE TO BE MORE CREATIVE. THE REAL CHALLENGE IS FINDING PLANT MATERIAL, BUT THAT ONLY MAKES THE HUNT MORE THRILLING. OFTEN THE PLANTS I'M LOOKING FOR, SUCH AS FALSE CYPRESS, HOLLIES, LEUCOTHOES, AND HELLEBORES, HAVE BEEN SHOVED BACK INTO PLASTIC-COVERED GREENHOUSES FOR SAFEKEEPING UNTIL SPRING.

At one point in early winter, I was faced with pulling together my house and garden for a hastily planned party. It was after Thanksgiving, but well before Christmas. I wanted to greet my guests with some containers near my entryway, so I dashed out to see what I could find. After wading through a sea of cut Christmas trees, I unearthed some three-gallon pots of deciduous holly. The tall spires of their red-berried stems were as bright as a new fire truck. Next, I found some small creeping junipers and a couple of nice white flowering kale left over from the autumn season along with some variegated ivy. I bought enough plants to fill four frostproof pots, rushed home, and threw them together. I even surprised myself with the results.

Winter is also the time I enjoy creating planted containers for the interior of my house. There are several colorful varieties of winter-blooming flowers such as cyclamen and orchids that combine beautifully with ferns, ivy, and other houseplants to make long-lasting indoor displays. I also pot up lots of paperwhite bulbs in everything from soup tureens to ceramic bowls. By planting several bulbs each week from Thanksgiving until Christmas I enjoy a continuous bloom of fresh flowers through the month of January. Indoors and out, winter containers add beauty to the garden home.

A cast-iron container is a safe bet in winter. It can take freezing temperatures without cracking. Filled with cold-tolerant plants, this combination is undaunted by a light snow.

SUN • Garden Home Principle: **FOCAL POINT**

52. False Cypress and Yellow Dogwood

Blast away the winter blues with some bright foliage plants that can tolerate the cold and still look great. Choose a prominent location for this container where you can enjoy viewing its beauty from inside. The design can work as an eye-catching centerpiece in a garden room with a loose, informal style and equally as well in a more formal setting. Consider placing it against a bank of ornamental grasses. The neutral colors and fine texture of the foliage make a wonderful backdrop. Another striking setting would be in front of a dark green boxwood.

1   dark green cast-iron container—18 inches deep × 24 inches diameter (with 19-inch inside diameter)
1   2-gallon 'Templehof' Hinoki false cypress (*Chamaecyparis obtusa* 'Templehof')
1   2-gallon 'Flaviramea' yellow twig dogwood (*Cornus sericea* 'Flaviramea')
1   1-gallon 'Rainbow' leucothoe (*Leucothoe fontanesiana* 'Rainbow')
1   1-gallon 'Golden Baby' ivy (*Hedera helix* 'Golden Baby')
2   1-quart 'Ogon' sweet flag acorus (*Acorus gramineus* 'Ogon')

After the holidays and before things start getting busy outdoors, I enjoy browsing through local antiques stores to see what treasures I might unearth for my garden. I was immediately attracted to this large cast-iron container as soon as I spied it in a friend's shop. Its dark green color seemed to reflect the somber tones of the winter landscape and since it was metal, I knew it could tolerate the cold without cracking.

After loading it into the car, a challenge in itself because of its immense weight, I headed for the nursery to see what they had left in their plant inventory. I found a nice assortment of coniferous evergreens. These plants are a good choice for a winter arrangement because they are less likely to be damaged by the wind, snow, or cold weather. I figure that if an evergreen is tough enough to live outdoors in the winter, it's a good bet that I can grow it in a container. I also chose a pot of yellow twig dogwoods along with some leucothoe, ivy, and acorus.

The composition plays the yellow branches of the dogwood against the evergreen foliage of the cypress. This high contrast enhances the appearance of both plants. The dogwood also serves as the tall, spiky form of the design.

The long golden leaves of the perennial herb sweet flag acorus replicate the lines of the dogwood. Snuggled in between the cypress and the acorus is 'Rainbow' leucothoe, which helps to warm things up with its colorful leaves in shades of deep red, pink, yellow, green, and copper. For the cascading element in the arrangement, yellow variegated ivy tumbles over the edge to finish the design.

Plant List
A. *'Templehof' Hinoki false cypress*
B. *'Flaviramea' yellow twig dogwood*
C. *'Rainbow' leucothoe*
D. *'Golden Baby' ivy*
E. *'Ogon' sweet flag acorus*

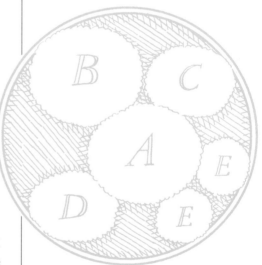

things to keep in mind
* Use a weatherproof container.
* High contrast in plant forms and color heightens interest in the composition.
* Replant shrubs in a garden border in the spring.

DUSTY MILLER

'ICE FOLLIES' DAFFODIL

'BLUE STAR' JUNIPER

'PENNY WHITE' VIOLA

LAVENDER COTTON

• No. 58 •

53. Blue Juniper and Gray Santolinas

Highlight the entrance to your house or garden with this seasonal accent. A pair of these containers makes an even stronger statement, with plants inspired by the soft, frosty blue color and wintry look of the urn.

1   light blue cast-iron urn—21 inches tall × 26 inches diameter (with 21-inch inside diameter)
2   2-gallon 'Blue Star' juniper (*Juniperus squamata* 'Blue Star')
2   1-gallon lavender cotton (*Santolina chamaecyparissus*)
2   6-packs 'Penny White' viola (*Viola cornuta* 'Penny White')
6–8 3-inch pots dusty miller (*Centaurea cineraria*)
7   bulbs 'Ice Follies' daffodil (*Narcissus* sp.)

Plant List
A. *'Blue Star' juniper*
B. *Lavender cotton*
C. *'Penny White' viola*
D. *Dusty miller*
E. *'Ice Follies' daffodil*

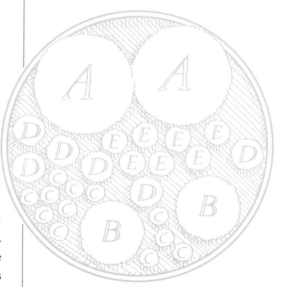

You never know when you are going to stumble on a new addition to your garden. I spotted this late-nineteenth-century cast-iron urn at a church garden show. I was immediately attracted to its worn look and frosty blue color. It was one of those serendipitous finds when I wasn't looking for a container, but I knew if I didn't get it, I would have wished that I had.

I was eager to try using some daffodils in this arrangement. While some people have luck planting bulbs directly in containers, I prefer to plant them in the fall in spare plastic nursery pots and keep them in my lathe house until they are up and growing. In late winter, I plant the rest of the arrangement and leave room in the back for the bulbs. After the threat of below-freezing temperatures passes, I tuck the emerging bulbs in the container with the other plants.

The silvery gray colors of these plants work well with the cool blue container to create a perfect winter arrangement. The powdery gray foliage of the dusty miller echoes the urn's patina and is picked up by the gray-green santolinas. The urn's blue theme is also echoed by the 'Blue Star' junipers.

All-white and cream-colored flowers of the violas and daffodils keep the arrangement looking crisp and clean. Even before the 'Ice Follies' daffodils open, their blue-gray foliage harmonizes with the arrangement's color scheme. After they bloom, remove the spent blossoms and leave the foliage in place. As the season turns to spring, refresh the container by removing the daffodils and adding some potted tulips.

Violas are the perfect flowering plant for winter containers because they will bloom in low light and cool temperatures, performing even better than pansies. They have the amazing capacity to freeze solid and then become revived again. The 'Penny' viola series is particularly steadfast under winter's trying conditions.

things to keep in mind

* Tightly drawn compositions are better suited for winter containers. Save fine foliage and loose arrangements for spring and summer.
* Winter containers need to be watered. Plants are better prepared to endure an extended cold spell if they are well hydrated.
* This arrangement does best in a sunny, protected area.

SUN • Garden Home Principle: **SHAPE AND FORM**

54. Winter Whites in Black Trough

The long shape of this black metal trough is well suited for a design reminiscent of a miniature landscape. The arrangement has a casual nature, but lends an air of sophistication to a setting with its somewhat formal white and green color scheme. An ideal setting for this container would be on a terrace just outside a white room, helping to extend the interior colors outdoors.

1   black metal trough—24 inches long × 10 inches wide × 16 inches deep
1   2-gallon dwarf Alberta spruce (*Picea glauca* 'Conica')
1   1-gallon 'Ingelise' variegated ivy (*Hedera helix* 'Ingelise')
2   6- packs 'Crown White' pansy (*Viola × wittrockiana* 'Crown White')
3   1-quart 'Silver Dragon' lilyturf (*Liriope spicata* 'Silver Dragon')
5   3-inch pots 'Emperor' flowering kale (*Brassica oleracea* 'Emperor')
3   3-inch pots 'White Crane' flowering kale (*Brassica oleracea* 'White Crane')
5   paperwhite bulbs (*Narcissus*)

I found this black trough on a visit to New York City's Flower District while looking for some glass vases. I happened into a shop that carried a line of these contemporary-style containers made of tin. They came in several sizes and I liked the shape, so I had a few shipped home.

   This arrangement was designed to look like a miniature landscape in the long trough. A dwarf Alberta spruce at the far end of the container starts to build a sense of perspective in the composition. This evergreen is a good choice for the winter because it is cold hardy and has a compact, columnar form. The spruce sits tall in the pocket-sized landscape with the other plants stepping down in size just as you often see in flower borders.

   The spruce also serves as a dark backdrop for the paperwhite narcissus, complementing the cream-colored blooms and gray-green foliage. These heavenly scented clusters of flowers are a joy to grow indoors or out.

Plant List
A. *Dwarf Alberta spruce*
B. *'Ingelise' variegated ivy*
C. *'Crown White' pansy*
D. *'Silver Dragon' lilyturf*
E. *'Emperor' flowering kale*
F. *'White Crane' flowering kale*
G. *Paperwhite bulbs*

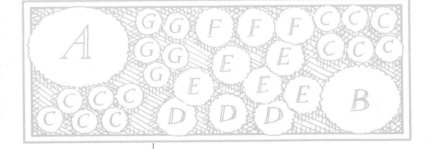

things to keep in mind
* Create the feel of a miniature landscape in trough-shaped containers.
* Dark backdrops set off brightly colored flowers.
* Check with local nurseries for the best cold-hardy plants for your area.

'CROWN WHITE' PANSY

DWARF ALBERTA SPRUCE

PAPERWHITE BULBS

'WHITE CRANE' FLOWERING KALE

'SILVER DRAGON' LILYTURF

'INGELISE' VARIEGATED IVY

'EMPEROR' FLOWERING KALE

• No. 54 •

SUN • Garden Home Principle: **ENCLOSURE**

55. Pink Heather and Blue-Gray Evergreens

A series of these troughs evenly spaced around the edge of a deck or terrace gives the area stylish protection with a low border that defines the space but doesn't obstruct the view. The complementary forms in this arrangement, all mounded together, make a nice, rolling silhouette. Combining a juniper with a mixture of cold-hardy flowers and foliage creates a long-lasting display that only improves through the season.

1	gray fiberglass trough—26 inches long × 12 inches wide × 12 inches deep
1	2-gallon 'Blue Star' juniper (*Juniperus squamata* 'Blue Star')
1	6-inch pot 'Mediterranean Pink' heather (*Erica* × *darleyensis* 'Mediterranean Pink')
1	1-quart 'Bath's Pink' dianthus (*Dianthus gratianopolitanus* 'Bath's Pink')
1	4-inch pot purple kale (*Brassica oleracea* 'Acephala')
3	3-inch pots dusty miller (*Centaurea cineraria*)
3	3-inch pots purple cabbage (*Brassica oleracea*)
1	6-pack 'Penny Violet Flare' viola (*Viola cornuta* 'Penny Violet Flare')

Plant List

A. *'Blue Star' juniper*
B. *'Mediterranean Pink' heather*
C. *'Bath's Pink' dianthus*
D. *Purple kale*
E. *Dusty miller*
F. *Purple cabbage*
G. *'Penny Violet Flare' viola*

When I first reached for this rectangular trough at a local garden center, I thought it was a lead box and was expecting it to be of a hefty weight. Instead, it almost flew off the shelf. It was actually made of a fiberglass resin material weighing less than six pounds. I must confess that when these new lightweight containers were first introduced, I was not impressed. They seemed obviously artificial and stuck out in a garden like a sore thumb. But recent manufacturing improvements have turned out better reproductions and some, like this one, are so good that they helped me overcome my initial reluctance. Since these fiberglass containers are frostproof, they are ideal for gardens with below-freezing temperatures. And I haven't found their composition to adversely affect the growth or health of the plants.

The leaden color of this container captures the mood of the season. Ornamental cabbage and kale (leftover from the fall planting season) combine beautifully with the purple violas, creating a medley of jewel tones brightened by the saturated pinks of the heather. Heather is great to combine with broad-leaf foliage plants like the kale because of the strong contrast in plant forms. The gray tones in the dusty miller, juniper, and dianthus echo the color of the container and help pull together all the elements.

In a full-sun location and with regular watering on frost-free days, the arrangement just gets better and better. As the daylight hours increase, the violas perk up and the kale expands; by spring, the dianthus will be in full bloom, providing months of enjoyment.

things to keep in mind

* Fiberglass is frostproof and a good choice for winter containers.
* If you can't find the exact size of plant called for in the recipe, assemble the equivalent by juxtaposing two plants. To create a natural look, combine a larger plant with a smaller one rather than two same-size plants.

56. Snapdragons and English Daisies Illuminated with Golden Foliage

This design makes a great eye-catching centerpiece in a garden. When framed by an archway or gate, the lively colors and bold shape of the container create an enticing attraction that will draw visitors deeper into your garden. By using a tall, classically shaped urn, nature will not only be near, but lifted to eye level.

1 gray cast-iron urn—29 inches tall × 22 inches diameter (with 17-inch inside diameter)
1 3-gallon five color false holly (*Osmanthus heterophyllus* 'Goshiki')
3 6-inch 'Floral Showers Fuchsia' snapdragon (*Antirrhinum majus* 'Floral Showers Fuchsia')
1 6-inch hanging basket 'Golden Baby' ivy (*Hedera helix* 'Golden Baby')
2 1-quart dark pink English daisy (*Bellis perennis*)
2 1-quart light pink English daisy (*Bellis perennis*)
2 6-packs 'Lemon Chiffon Sorbet' viola (*Viola cornuta* 'Lemon Chiffon Sorbet')

One design trick I've discovered is that if you want to give a winter container a spark of energy, add yellow. It always astonishes me what a difference it makes. When the winter sun hangs low in the sky and our eyes search for any bright spot of light, splashes of yellow in a grouping of plants can be a real spirit lifter. The spiky golden yellow stems of the false holly osmanthus and the softer lemon yellow violas in this recipe add a rich vibrancy to the arrangement.

The inspiration for this color combination begins with the yellow centers of the pink-petaled English daisies. 'Lemon Chiffon Sorbet' violas play off that bright eye, and are the perfect match. The osmanthus echo the yellow and serve as a bright backdrop for all of the pink flowers. The two tones of pink daisies mix light and dark colors to make the composition look less contrived.

English daisies have been part of American gardens since the 1700s. Thomas Jefferson noted in his journals that they grew in the "open ground on the west" at Monticello. You may know them by one of their common names: herb Margaret, bone flower, or my favorite, measure of love.

To achieve a mature look that matches the rest of the composition, split a hanging basket of yellow-variegated ivy and tuck it along the edges of the container so its long tendrils trail over the sides. The deeply saturated fuchsia snapdragons add a richness and depth to the arrangement.

Plant List
A. Five color false holly
B. 'Floral Showers Fuchsia' snapdragon
C. 'Golden Baby' ivy
D. Dark pink English daisy
E. Light pink English daisy
F. 'Lemon Chiffon Sorbet' viola

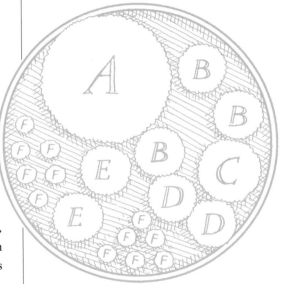

things to keep in mind

* To add sparkle to a winter container, use plants with yellow foliage and blooms. But don't overdo it; too much can be overwhelming.
* English daisies rebloom when spent flowers are removed.
* To move heavy containers safely, strap them into an appliance cart or onto a dolly.

FIVE COLOR FALSE HOLLY

LIGHT PINK ENGLISH DAISY

'FLORAL SHOWERS FUCHSIA' SNAPDRAGON

'LEMON CHIFFON SORBET' VIOLA

'GOLDEN BABY' IVY

DARK PINK ENGLISH DAISY

• No. 56 •

SUN • Garden Home Principle: **SHAPE AND FORM**

57. Winter Trio

The more, the merrier. A communal arrangement of containers is a great way to gain more visual impact and create a design that feels like a landscape. This would make a great little rooftop garden. Place the containers close to your house so you can enjoy seeing them from indoors. This ensemble shines on a bright winter day.

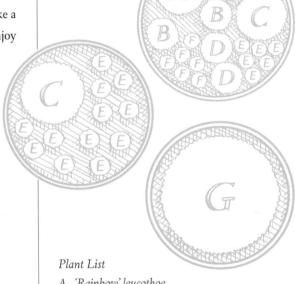

3   black metal containers
- Container #1—19 inches diameter × 16 inches deep
- Container #2—16 inches diameter × 14 inches deep
- Container #3—16 inches diameter × 14 inches deep

CONTAINER #1

2   1-gallon 'Rainbow' leucothoe (*Leucothoe fontanesiana* 'Rainbow')
2   6-inch pots 'Mediterranean Pink' heather (*Erica* × *darleyensis* 'Mediterranean Pink')
1   1-gallon 'Blue Star' juniper (*Juniperus squamata* 'Blue Star')
2   1-quart purple cabbage (*Brassica oleracea*)
1   6-pack 'Lemon Chiffon Sorbet' viola (*Viola cornuta* 'Lemon Chiffon Sorbet')
1   6-pack 'Sorbet Blue Heaven' Viola (*Viola cornuta* 'Sorbet Blue Heaven')

CONTAINER #2

1   1-gallon 'Blue Star' juniper (*Juniperus squamata* 'Blue Star')
2   6-packs 'Lemon Chiffon Sorbet' viola (*Viola cornuta* 'Lemon Chiffon Sorbet')

CONTAINER #3

1   5-gallon margaritaville yucca (*Yucca recurvifolia* 'Hinvargus')

Plant List

A. *'Rainbow' leucothoe*
B. *'Mediterranean Pink' heather*
C. *'Blue Star' juniper*
D. *Purple cabbage*
E. *'Lemon Chiffon Sorbet' viola*
F. *'Sorbet Blue Heaven' viola*
G. *Margaritaville yucca*

In winter we often depend on a plant's texture and form more than its bloom to create visual interest. This arrangement is a variation on my Three-Shape Rule of mixing three plant forms—tall and spiky, round and full, trailing or cascading—into one container. Here, instead of using just one container, a trio of planters works together to express these forms.

A large yellow variegated yucca dominates one container and serves as the tall and spiky element. The other pots in the ensemble are filled with round and cascading forms. Contrasting shapes and textures bring interest to these containers. The thick, leathery leaves of the ornamental cabbage add weight and texture against the finer foliage of the juniper and heather in the large container. The 'Blue Star' juniper and the 'Lemon Chiffon Sorbet' violas are used again in the smaller pot. The cadence created by repeating the plant varieties and the color yellow helps knit together the composition.

A secret of combining several pots is to arrange an odd number of containers collectively in a grouping. Use one container that is large and dominating, another that fills in the middle, and one that's low to the ground. These staggered heights produce pleasing combinations. It is also easier to unify the design when all of the containers are the same color or made of the same material. But this isn't a hard and fast rule. Don't shy away from using differing container styles. A certain level of harmony can be achieved by using plants that flow together and unite the overall design.

things to keep in mind

* Bold groupings make a strong visual impact in a winter landscape.
* Cluster together odd numbers (3, 5, 7) of containers.
* Larger containers are less prone to freezing solid due to more soil volume.

'VALLEY ROSE' JAPANESE ANDROMEDA

RED TWIG DOGWOOD

'EVERGOLD' SEDGE

'HARBOUR DWARF' NANDINA

'NEEDLEPOINT' IVY

• No. 58 •

SUN • Garden Home Principle: **ENTRY**

58. Red-Stemmed Winter Ensemble

There is nothing like red to grab your eye in winter. Red-toned leaves and stems mix and mingle in this design to create a warm and welcoming accent to a home's front door or as a bold highlight to usher guests through the entrance of your garden. Use containers to draw attention to your entries and foreshadow a sense of your style.

1   Italian terra-cotta container—24 inches diameter × 20 inches deep

1   3-gallon red twig dogwood (*Cornus sericea*)

2   1-gallon 'Valley Rose' Japanese andromeda (*Pieris japonica* 'Valley Rose')

3   1-gallon 'Harbour Dwarf' nandina (*Nandina domestica* 'Harbour Dwarf')

3   1-quart 'Needlepoint' ivy (*Hedera helix* 'Needlepoint')

2   1-gallon 'Evergold' sedge (*Carex hachijoensis* 'Evergold')

Having grown up in the nursery business, I was accustomed to seeing stacks of dormant, bare-root trees and shrubs stored in coolers during the winter. What may have seemed like harsh treatment was actually harmless to the plants as long as their roots were kept moist and cool. Last January, when I found this red twig dogwood in a large three-gallon pot, I knew that I could wash most of the soil from the roots, place it in my twenty-four-inch-diameter terra-cotta container, and still have room for the other plants and soil.

A Japanese andromeda was added to match the cerise buds and dark red stems of the dogwood. The mature leaves of this broadleaf evergreen shrub are a glossy dark green, but the new growth is a bronzy pink to red. Building on the red theme, the 'Harbor Dwarf' nandina with its bright reddish purple foliage adds even more depth to the composition. While red is a warm color in winter, it can also be rather somber, so this arrangement is offset with a spot of yellow in the grasslike foliage of the variegated Japanese sedge 'Evergold'. The green ivy cascading down the front is a nice complement to the reds in the arrangement and also plays off of the nandina foliage.

This is a durable combination of foliage plants with no tender blooms, so it can tolerate cold temperatures and still look great. If you can't find a red twig dogwood, then a yellow twig dogwood or any of the salix pussy willows will also work. A yellow variegated ivy can replace the green variety or act as a substitute for the Japanese sedge 'Evergold'.

Plant List

A. *Red twig dogwood*

B. *'Valley Rose' Japanese andromeda*

C. *'Harbour Dwarf' nandina*

D. *'Evergold' sedge*

E. *'Needlepoint' ivy*

things to keep in mind

✳ Look to foliage plants for color in winter containers.

✳ When mixing similar colors, it is important to choose plants that will contrast each other in leaf size, texture, or form so each will be noticed.

✳ A rule of thumb to keep the composition in balance is that plants should be no more than one and a half times the height of the container.

✳ One note of caution: when using terra-cotta containers in winter, don't put saucers under the pots to collect water because if the water freezes, it can damage the container.

59. White Orchids and Cyclamen

Bring the garden inside with this slice of paradise. Orchids suggest faraway exotic places, a nice thought in the midst of winter. For a clean start after the holidays, white flowers help kick off the year in a bright way—always refreshing after the glitter of seasonal celebrations. This simple monochromatic theme will fit in comfortably with most interiors, and is particularly striking as an entry-hall arrangement to greet guests, whether on a round center table or on a sideboard below a mirror.

1   green ceramic jardinière—18 inches diameter × 8 inches deep
2   5-inch pots white moth orchid (*Phalaenopsis* hybrids)
3   1-quart 'Sassy' Boston fern (*Nephrolepis exaltata* 'Sassy')
3   4-inch pots 'Miracle White' mini cyclamen (*Cyclamen persicum* 'Miracle White')
1   1-gallon 'Glacier' English ivy (*Hedera helix* 'Glacier')

All the plants in this combination are long-lasting and hold up quite well indoors, providing enjoyment for weeks. Depending on the style of your home, a simple orchid may be all you need for a more minimalist look. If you prefer a more gardenlike statement, mix foliage with flowers.

When I am creating an interior container, I tailor the design a little more carefully to the setting. While color is important outside, it takes on a more notable quality in an interior room. It is important for there to be a close association between the colors of the composition and the colors of the décor.

The *Phalaenopsis* orchid is a striking plant that's hard to resist. They are readily available and if cared for properly, they will bloom for months. The white cyclamen runs a close second to the orchid as far as having long-lasting flowers. In this arrangement, the dark backdrop of the Boston ferns' green foliage helps to better illuminate the cyclamen's blooms. 'Glacier' ivy's creamy white variegations repeat the white theme of the orchid and cyclamen as it tumbles down the front of the container. Just that little touch of white around the margins is enough to reflect the color of the flowers and ground the arrangement. The soft gray-green ceramic jardinière container blends softly with the white monochromatic theme.

Rather than planting the pots in soil, they can be placed in their nursery pots or transferred to plastic sandwich bags and placed into the ceramic container, using blocks of Styrofoam to elevate each plant to the desired height. For added vitality, thoroughly presoak each plant before placing it in the larger container. Cover the tops of the nursery pots with sphagnum moss to give the arrangement a finished look.

Plant List
A. *White moth orchid*
B. *'Sassy' Boston fern*
C. *'Miracle White' mini cyclamen*
D. *'Glacier' English ivy*

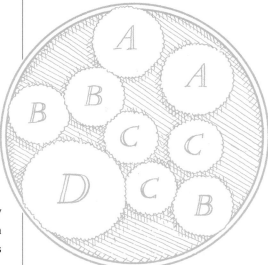

things to keep in mind
* Place the container in indirect or filtered light.
* Containers with wide openings are best suited for these arrangements.
* Check the plants for signs of spider mites such as masses of tiny spiderwebs and mottled yellow foliage.

INTERIOR • Garden Home Principle: **WHIMSY**

6o. Pink and Salmon Cyclamen with Ferns

Add a little fun to your kitchen or breakfast table with this tub of charming cyclamens. The petals are folded back and look as though they were surprised by a gust of wind. Broad shallow basins with wide openings work well for this type of design and chances are you already have a similar container on hand.

I	oval metal container with floral decal— 18 inches long × 13 inches wide × 10 inches deep
I	1-gallon maidenhair fern (*Adiantum* spp.)
I	6-inch pot 'Laser Pink Flame' cyclamen (*Cyclamen persicum intermediat* 'Laser Pink Flame')
3	4-inch pots 'Laser Salmon' cyclamen (*Cyclamen persicum intermediat* 'Laser Salmon')
2	3-inch pots purple waffle plant (*Pilea cadierii*)

Cyclamen are bright, carefree plants perfect for winter arrangements because they will bloom for a long time, often up to four months. They thrive and flourish at times of the year when there are fewer hours of daylight, making them ideal indoor houseplants.

The lively mix of pink and salmon cyclamens creates the focus of this arrangement. Using two closely related colors makes an interesting blend that matches the motif on the container. In addition to the blooms, the cyclamen's leaves make a statement of their own, taking on a hand-painted quality with their fine silver veining. For textural contrast, the crinkled foliage of a few purple waffle plants plays off the finely cut fronds of the maidenhair fern.

Plant List
A. *Maidenhair fern*
B: *'Laser Pink Flame' cyclamen*
C. *'Laser Salmon' cyclamen*
D. *Purple waffle plant*

things to keep in mind

❋ To keep the cyclamen healthy and happy, make sure they are well watered. Their weak point is along the stem by the flower head, so once that area withers, the flowers won't stand up.

❋ Three plants with contrasting foliage make a great-looking arrangement. Experiment with other houseplant choices to create new displays.

'LASER SALMON' CYCLAMEN

MAIDENHAIR FERN

'LASER PINK FLAME' CYCLAMEN

PURPLE WAFFLE PLANT

• No. 60 •

The Well-Appointed
POTTiNG ShED

Having a special area where I can work on container designs adds a lot to the enjoyment of putting them together. Tucked behind a clipped hornbeam arch in the corner of my property is a fenced-in area that serves as my outdoor utility room. This service yard is bordered on the north by my garage wall and on the east by an alley that runs along the back of my property. This location makes it convenient to drive down the alley and unload plants and materials at my work station. It is a concealed area where I can stack and store things and, frankly, make a big mess without having to keep it tidy for company.

Within this area I have a lathe house, or potting shed, where I pot containers and overwinter plants. The back of the shed is against the garage wall, which gives added protection. The walls are open lattice, allowing for air circulation in summer. As temperatures dip, I cover the walls with heavy plastic sheeting, which is enough to get my semihardy plants through the cold weather in my mid-South garden.

Creating a Work Space

Inside the potting shed I have a long workbench and various storage areas. If you've ever rubbed your aching back after bending over containers all day, you'll appreciate the joys of a potting bench. The surface is the height of a kitchen counter, so it's perfect for work that I do while standing up.

Now, I realize that not everyone has the room for such a setup, but even if you have limited space, you might be surprised with what you can find if you just look around for a spot. You could use a wall that is in or outside of your garage, a table on a covered porch or patio, or even a wide board mounted on a fence or along the side of your house in an inconspicuous location. All you really need is a place to mount some shelves or set up a table.

To create a potting area in my vegetable garden, I added a fold-down shelf on the side of my tool shed. When I need a work space, I lift the board and position the support braces to hold it securely in place.

Another place I like to work when the weather allows is on the loggia, or covered breezeway, between my house and garage. I often use the area as an outdoor dining area, so I like to keep it looking nice. To allow it to be used for multiple purposes, I converted a wooden armoire into a storage cupboard for my containers. With the doors closed, no one knows it is filled with a variety of pots and gardening supplies. When I'm ready to use it as a potting station, I just cover the outdoor dining table with newspaper and use it as my potting bench.

STOCKING THE POTTING SHED

A well-supplied potting shed is like a well-stocked pantry. Having all the equipment and tools you'll need close by makes it a pleasure to plant and maintain your containers. To give you an idea of the items needed to stock your shed, here is my list of potting essentials:

- *P. Allen Smith's Garden Home Journal* to record plant dates, varieties, and progress of containers
- Covered bins or other plastic storage containers with lids to hold potting soil mix, perlite, mulch, and fertilizers. While it is sometimes easier to just pile up these supplies in the bags they come in, I find my work space stays more organized and accessible when I create designated containers to hold these materials.
- Scoops for each bin
- Hand trowel for planting and transplanting
- Hand pruners and scissors to groom and thin plants
- Labels and an indelible pen to mark plants
- Fertilizer
- An assortment of containers in which to plant the finished arrangements
- Watering can
- Spray bottle
- Water hose and watering wand with fine-spray attachment
- Hand broom and dust pan to clean up work area
- Green gardener's twine to tie up climbing vines
- An assortment of large buckets to hold soil mixes while planting
- Large tubs or trays to collect spills during planting
- Measuring cups and spoons
- Plastic pots of various sizes to start seeds or hold plants from other containers
- Wheelbarrow for mixing soil blends
- Bamboo poles, stakes, trellis, and ties
- Gloves
- Potting soil, sand, ground bark mulch, and bagged garden soil

Container Fundamentals

EXTERIOR CONTAINER DESIGN

The real fun in selecting container recipes for your home starts with imagining where they will add the most beauty and style to your garden. Think of the containers as you would pieces of furniture or accessories inside your home. In some cases, they are the center of attention, the first thing you notice when you walk into a room. Or, they can work quietly to blend and harmonize with other elements of the décor. In that same way, you can place containers to play either starring or supporting roles in developing the look of your garden.

It is easy to fall into a rather predictable pattern of using containers as matching pairs at entries, or clustered in a grouping on patios and decks. To offer you some new ideas on how to incorporate containers in fun and compelling ways, I've listed the 12 Principles of Design outlined in my first book, *P. Allen Smith's Garden Home*. These basic elements are the guides that I always use to fashion gardens for my clients. The principles are repeated here to offer examples of how those same elements can be expressed in your garden design using planted containers.

Review the list and imagine how you might incorporate these elements to enhance your garden. You can also refer to the principle of design listed with each container recipe and the suggestions I offer for how to place the container in the landscape.

PRINCIPLE OF DESIGN	CONTAINER EXAMPLE
ENCLOSURE	Grow vining plants on lattice anchored between two containers to create a sense of enclosure.
SHAPE AND FORM	Define a formal or informal garden style through the shape and form of plants used in containers.
FRAMING THE VIEW	Plant window boxes beneath windows to frame views inside and outside your home.
ENTRY	Place matching containers at the entrances of your home and garden to offer a splendid reception.
FOCAL POINT	Create drama and instant attention with a well-placed, eye-catching container of striking plants.
STRUCTURE	Extend the style of your home's architecture into the garden with complementary styled containers.
COLOR	Harmonize your home's color scheme with coordinating containers and plants.
TEXTURE, PATTERN, AND RHYTHM	Use carefully selected combinations of plants in containers to create distinctive textures and patterns. Multiple containers placed at regular intervals develop a sense of rhythm in a garden's design.
ABUNDANCE	Develop a sense of abundance and generosity with containers full to overflowing in plants. Clusters of containers can add to that generous look.
WHIMSY	Add fun and playfulness with quirky plants or topiary in unusual containers.
MYSTERY	Build suspense and drama with large containers concealing bends in a path or areas of the garden.
TIME	Match the era of your home's style with plants and containers that mirror that time.

SELECTING THE RIGHT
CONTAINER FOR THE SETTING

Once you have identified the principles of design that you want to express with your planted container, the next step is to choose a complementary shape, size, and type of material for the container that will express those elements. This is an important part of the design process, so I'd like to offer some examples of how this works.

If you have a terrace where you need more privacy, applying the garden principle of enclosure to this area of your property would help. The idea would be to use containers along the perimeter of the terrace to create the suggestion of a wall or screen. There are many options you could choose, but by taking the lead from your house and selecting complementary materials, colors, and sizes that blend with your home's style, your best options will seem more apparent to you and the results more satisfying. If your house style is formal, planting several classic terra-cotta pots with tall Italian cypress and flowers could be a good harmonizing choice. For a more casual setting, wooden planter boxes filled with flowering lavender would be a nice pairing.

You will also want to factor in whether the container should stand out on its own as an accent or blend in with the plants. My best advice on this point is to think about how you intend to place the container within the landscape. For example, if you want to add some color accents in an established flowerbed and you don't want to disturb the bed, using a container that blends in discreetly but is brimming with bright flowers would be the best choice. The grouping of flowers become the "toss pillow" accessory to an otherwise styled setting, with the container acting as an inconspicuous holder. Like matching the right picture frame to a work of art, the container and the plants need to work together to achieve the total look.

CONTAINER SHAPES

There are several container shapes that act to suggest a certain style. Formal, urn-shaped vessels are best suited for like settings and would be out of place in a casual or rustic-style garden. Basket-weave planters are ideal for cottage gardens, bringing to mind armloads of flowers and a cozy, relaxed, and informal feel. The angular, clean lines of a footed planter suggest the serene landscape of an Asian garden. If you are in doubt which shape fits best in your setting, the safest best is to choose

CLASSIC

ASIAN

COTTAGE

FORMAL

a traditional terra-cotta pot. This classic shape works with any style.

Keep in mind that the container shape may limit the types of plants you can use in that pot. Some plants, such as small trees, shrubs, and perennials, have deep roots that require tall containers with enough depth to accommodate their long root masses. Annuals, on the other hand, often have fairly shallow roots and can thrive in low-profile containers.

Here are some descriptions of classic terra-cotta pots based on their height and width:

Long Tom—A container that is taller than it is wide, making it ideal for trailing plants. Good for deep-rooted plants such as trees and shrubs, but can be prone to tipping over.

Strawberry pot—A tall container with small pocket openings along the sides. Designed for herbs, strawberries, sedums, and other small flowering plants.

English pot—The classic slant-sided clay pot that comes in various dimensions, but is most often slightly taller than it is wide.

Standard pot—A container that is as tall as it is wide—a good selection for perennials.

Azalea pot—This container is three-fourths as tall as it is wide. It is a good choice for annuals, ferns, and shallow-rooted plants.

Bulb or pan pot—Half as tall as it is wide. Bulbs or other shallow-rooted plants such as sedums thrive in these pots.

Italian pot—A rimless container with a flared edge. Dimensions vary.

SCALE

Probably one of the most common mistakes gardeners make with their container gardens is selecting a pot that is too small in scale for its surroundings, so it becomes lost in the overall design. A successful design calls for a container to be proportional to its setting. While it is difficult to describe a hard and fast rule for you to follow in selecting a properly scaled container, my best advice is to look through garden-design magazines and books for good examples. Notice the size of the container and plants in relation to other objects in the photograph. If you find that a container you have already selected and planted is too small, consider clustering other containers around it for more visual mass. But keep in mind

that one or two well-scaled containers make a better statement than scattering around several smaller pots. Be sure to bring your tape measure with you as you shop for containers. Their sizes may be deceiving when out of context with your garden. Another way I like to get ideas is to visit well-designed gardens and take photos of good examples.

CONTAINER MATERIALS

After considering how the shape and size of the container affect its role in your garden's design, then you are ready to think about its construction. Clay, wood, metal, fiberglass, iron, copper, plastic, or even woven baskets are some of the more common container materials. There are several factors that may play a role in your selection, such as budget, if the container needs to be frostproof, ease or difficulty of moving it, which materials best match your garden's style, and where the container will be placed.

For example, if you want several large containers for a rooftop garden where the combined weight of the planters and the soil is a safety concern, choose those made from lightweight material such as plastic, fiberglass, or resin rather than stone or concrete. On the other hand, if the container will be in a windy location and the arrangement has several tall, large leafy plants, a heavy planter serves as a better anchor. Another consideration may be durability. If you intend to leave the container outside all year in temperatures below freezing, a planter that won't crack in cold weather is important. One type of frostproof terra-cotta called Italian impruneta is made from a gray clay dug from the Tuscan hills surrounding Impruneta, a small village nestled a few miles from Florence. Known as the most durable terra-cotta in the world, the pots can withstand temperatures down to twenty-two degrees below zero Fahrenheit.

As previously mentioned, materials as well as the size and shape of a container suggest certain styles. If your home is a formal pillared Colonial, wooden whiskey half barrels would not be the best complement to that period or design, just as overly ornate iron urns would be inappropriate with a rustic log cabin.

Here is a chart listing various materials and their qualities to help you select the best type for your situation.

CONTAINER MATERIAL	DURABILITY	WEIGHT	STYLE	COST
UNGLAZED TERRA-COTTA	Not frostproof, but a classic in temperate climates. Quality varies according to type of clay and how it was made. Soil dries out faster than in plastic pots due to clay's porous nature.	Depending on size, moderate. Very large containers can be quite heavy.	Universal in its classic style, fits in both formal and informal settings.	Generally low to moderate. Collectors pay high prices for specialty handmade pots or antiques.
ITALIAN IMPRUNETA TERRA-COTTA	The most durable type of terra-cotta. Frostproof. Able to withstand −22 degrees F.	Comparable to standard terra-cotta.	Distinctive pale pink coloration.	High—but worth it.
CERAMIC	Somewhat more durable than unglazed terra-cotta, due to glazing. Holds water and fertilizer longer as well.	Moderate, depending on sizes.	Often used in Asian and contemporary settings.	Moderate to high.
WOOD	Rugged, frost- and sunproof. Rot-resistant woods such as redwood, cedar, and cypress last longer. Others benefit from paint or waterproofing.	Moderate to heavy depending on type of wood, design, and size.	Varies widely depending on design. Twig containers and whiskey barrels are informal. Versailles boxes are formal.	Low to moderate.
CONCRETE/ PRECAST	Very durable, withstands sun and frost. However, with no drainage, can crack in extremely cold temperatures.	Very heavy—good anchors but not for areas where weight is a concern.	Versatile, can be poured into many styles of molds	Low to high.

CONTAINER MATERIAL	DURABILITY	WEIGHT	STYLE	COST
CAST IRON	With proper drainage, lasts forever. Fertilizers can cause corrosion.	Very heavy—challenging to move.	Common in Victorian and cottage-style gardens	High.
PLASTIC	Unless treated, has limited durability in both sun and frost. Check the label. Good as a liner for other containers. Retains moisture longer.	Lightweight.	If they are well designed and manufactured, can be mistaken for higher grade materials. Wide variety of styles, colors, and shapes for every setting.	Low to moderate.
RESIN/ FIBERGLASS	Frostproof. Check label for UV resistance.	Lightweight—easy to transport and move once planted.	Some are indistinguishable from terracotta, stone, or metal. Very versatile—in a variety of styles.	Moderate to high.
GALVANIZED METAL	Frostproof and sunproof. Be sure to add holes for drainage.	Lightweight.	Usually informal style—can be painted.	Low.
LEAD	Frostproof and very durable.	Very heavy.	Formal.	High.
CARVED STONE	Frostproof and sunproof. Often needs holes for drainage.	Very heavy.	Depending on design, either formal or informal.	High.

RECYCLED CONTAINERS

One of the best ways to add a whimsical touch to your garden is to use an unconventional holder as a container for your plantings. The best container may be an object that was never intended to hold plants at all. A pair of old work boots, a pot in the seat of a broken chair, red wagons, antique watering cans, wash tubs, milk cans, or just about anything that can hold soil can be used. The best places to find these items are in your attic, garage, or basement, or spend an afternoon poking around yard sales, thrift shops, and junk stores to find that special something.

COLOR

As you choose your container and plants, remember that no color is isolated in the garden. Every composition should be created while considering where it will be displayed in its immediate surroundings. The container may be placed on a high point against the blue sky, in front of a mass of dark green plants, near buildings, or next to garden ornaments and furnishings. Your color selections can make subtle changes or create strong attention-getting accents. For instance, the weathered patina of a classic terra-cotta pot can either blend quietly into the fabric of the garden or it can be painted a bright color to stand out.

This is truly a place to have fun and let your personal style come through. Many of the same color theories that apply to using color inside your home also hold true with containers and plants in your garden. Use bright primary colors such as red and yellow when you want the composition to visually advance, and rely on softer pastels, pinks, light purples, and blues when you wish to create the illusion of distance.

Complementary colors, such as yellow and blue, build visual interest. If you have an informal cottage-style garden replete with pale yellows and buttery creams, a pair of dull, chalky blue containers at the entrance might be just the right touch. Or if your taste leans toward the contemporary and your garden is a study in various shades of green, try a large red-glazed container as a focal point. If that seems too bold, try taking your lead from the color of the house or the trunks of surrounding trees. Grungy greens and grays are neutral hues that blend easily into a garden.

MODIFYING CONTAINER COLORS

If the bright orange of a new terra-cotta pot is too strong for your garden's color scheme, you can tone it down to help it settle comfortably into its setting. Toning down the color of terra-cotta and new concrete eliminates that bright edge which often competes with the colors of the plants. Apply a light wash of old-fashioned milk paint or try a nice dove gray exterior latex paint mixed 50/50 with water, then liberally apply it to the container with a brush. Before it dries, wipe off the excess with a rag. For a final touch (especially for concrete containers), grab a handful of grass or weeds and rub them on the surface. The effect magically ages a container, giving it a more natural look in the garden. Dull greens and taupe applied with a light hand can also neutralize the intense orange of new terra-cotta.

Glazing is another way to add and modify color in the garden. An ordinary strawberry jar can be transformed into a more sophisticated version of itself with a dark green, blue, or even black glaze. The dark, hard, glossy finish is an attractive juxtaposition for softer glaucous leaves of sedums and sempervivums.

A ready supply of various sizes and shapes of terra-cotta pots line the shelves of my potting shed.

{Aging a Container}

Turning brand-new garden ornaments and containers into 200-year-old masterpieces is surprisingly simple and, depending on their size, can be done in just a few minutes.

The English have a time-honored method for aging concrete that involves buttermilk and sheep manure. However, not everyone has the stomach for that. A much more pleasant way to achieve the same effect is with paint and water. This technique will work on both concrete and terra-cotta.

1. The first thing you want to do is get the paint right. I use a water-based latex exterior paint. When it comes to choosing a color, the grungier the better. I think a gray-green works great.

2. Next, dilute the paint with water, about half and half. The mixture should have the consistency of tomato soup.

3. Then just slop it on your containers with a paintbrush. Before it dries, wipe off the excess paint with a clean rag or damp sponge, leaving traces of color in the crevices.

4. Now the finishing touch and real secret to this technique is to rub down the container with some weeds or grass. The green juice helps blend the colors and makes the container look as if it has been outdoors for several seasons.

1.

2.

3.

4.

I.

2.

3.

{Cleaning Terra-Cotta Pots}

Sometimes it is necessary to clean terra-cotta pots to remove salt buildup from fertilizers and kill any pathogens to prevent passing disease from one planting season to the next. It is a simple task that can be done in an afternoon.

1. Inspect last season's terra-cotta containers and gather those that have a white, crusty buildup on their outer surfaces.

2. To clean used terra-cotta pots, place them in a large tub and soak them for about 30 minutes in a 10 percent bleach solution. Rince thoroughly in clean water.

3. In a saucer, make a paste mixing baking soda with a small amount of water and apply to the sides of the pot.

4. Use a stiff brush to scrub off the paste and remove the salt buildup. Rinse with clean water.

4.

{Waterproofing Containers}

If you've priced containers lately, you know they can be quite an investment. If you choose terra-cotta, stone, concrete, or other porous materials, they can also be quite fragile, so it just makes good sense to take care of them. These materials are particularly vulnerable during the winter when water is absorbed into the surface. When temperatures drop, the water freezes and expands, and the container can crack. An effective preventative measure is to apply a water sealer.

- Simply brush a generous amount of water sealer on the inside of the container and around the outside of the lip. You can use any commercial wood sealer.
- Allow the sealer to dry completely before adding potting soil.

SELECTING PLANTS AT THE GARDEN CENTER

With your container and plant recipe in mind, make a list of plants you will need to create your design. The most important consideration at this stage is the light conditions where you will place the container. For example, choosing a shade plant design for a full-sun location is a recipe for disaster.

You may also find that you need to modify the ingredients a bit considering the plants available in your area. As suggested before, qualified garden center personnel should be able to help you find plants that are similar in color, form, and size as well as light requirements, as substitutions. Adaptations may also be required in the number of plants if you use a different container size, or if you simply want to add your own creative flair to the arrangement.

As you make your plant selections at the garden center, look for plants that appear healthy, vigorous, and well cared for. Avoid those that are wilted or have yellow leaves.

Without harming the plant, gently slide it out of the container and check for healthy roots that are white, firm, and not root-bound in the pot.

Plants are often packed together to save bench space at a nursery, so pull out several of the same plant and put them in your cart. This will give you a chance to inspect each one and choose the healthiest specimens.

To get an idea of how the color, forms, and textures will work together, you may find it helpful to take all the plants you want to use in the design to an area where you can group them together and arrange them as they will appear in the container. This approach is no different from decorating a room in your home where you assemble the various fabrics, wall covers, and paint samples to get an idea of how they will work together.

PLANTING BASICS

Now that you have your container and plants, here are some guidelines to follow before you put your arrangements together.

LIGHT CONDITIONS

Once again, make sure that you have selected plants that will thrive in the light conditions for the area where you will be placing the container. Note that some recipes were designed for full to partial shade settings, while others were created for full to partial sun locations. This is important if you want your container plantings to thrive.

DRAINAGE

It is essential that your plants have adequate drainage. Few grow well with "wet feet" in soppy soil. Most manufactured containers have drainage holes that give water an escape route through the soil and out the bottom of the container. If your planter does not, you may need to drill or punch holes in the bottom to make sure water does not collect in the base. If an electric drill is used, a masonry bit may be needed for clay or concrete containers. To prevent the soil from escaping, place broken pot shards, a shallow layer of gravel, or even a small piece of window screen over the drainage holes.

Good drainage is essential to the vitality of container plants. If necessary, drill holes in the bottom of pots using an electric drill with the appropriate bit (for masonry, wood, or metal).

DRIP TRAYS

Drip trays or container saucers are important for baskets, window boxes, containers suspended over doorways, or containers placed wherever stains from escaping water might be a problem. A drip tray can be a simple saucer under a terra-cotta pot or a reservoir and drip chamber within the container. Sometimes a large single tray filled with gravel or pebbles can serve as a reservoir for several containers. Another option is to set one container with drainage holes inside a container that does not have drainage holes. If you use this technique, put a layer of gravel in the bottom of the outer container and set the container with holes inside it on top of the gravel. Plants that require additional humidity often benefit from this, as the collected water in the gravel evaporates upward, through the leaves of the plants.

SOIL MIXES

Virtually all of the plants recommended in my container designs will thrive when planted in a packaged container soil mix. These highly engineered growing media have been developed to give your plants everything they need. Resist the temptation to dig up your garden soil for the containers. Even the best soil is often contaminated with weed seeds, insects, and fungal diseases that will quickly infect your containers.

When shopping for soil mixes at your local garden center, you may find them categorized as potting soil, soil-less mix, container mix, growing mix, or growing media. Avoid packaged soil labeled as topsoil or compost. Those are not formulated for containers. When it comes to which brand is best, my advice is to try one, and if it does well for you, stick with it. The brand I have found reliable over the years is Premier Pro-Mix container soil.

There are different grades of soil container mixes, such as standard and premium. Standard mixes offer basic elements that will sustain your plant's growth but do not have the extras the premium mixes offer such as fertilizer, wetting agents, and water-retentive polymers. Check the labels for ingredients so you know what you are getting for your money.

PLANTING TECHNIQUES

After you gather all your plants, potting mix, and the container, you are ready to plant. If the container is large, heavy, or difficult to transport, you should plant it where it will be displayed. Otherwise, plant the container in the potting shed or other location where water and soil spills won't be a problem, then move it to its new location.

In general, there are three basic types of containers featured in this book: pots, window boxes, and hanging baskets. The following are some basic guidelines to follow for all containers, with some specific tips for each type.

First, the general guidelines:

START WITH CLEAN CONTAINERS

If the container is new, simply wipe it with a soft cloth to remove any debris. If you are reusing a pot from a previous season, remove all the old soil and use a stiff brush to clean out the container. For terra-cotta, glazed ceramic, plastic, or other washable surfaces, use a weak bleach solution—one teaspoon per gallon of water—and let the container soak for an hour or so, then thoroughly rinse and let it air dry.

WEIGHT REDUCTION

There are light and superlight soil mixes for situations where the weight of the container may be a safety issue. The weight of a heavy container may put undue stress on a balcony, a rooftop, a window box, or areas of decks away from supporting posts. A one-foot-square container filled with wet planting soil can weigh fifty pounds. A fifty-gallon container designed for a tree will weigh several hundred pounds. Be sure to choose the appropriate container and soil mix for the situation.

One trick I have employed for weight reduction is to place a garbage bag of packing peanuts in the base of large containers. If I don't need all that room for tree or shrub roots, this fills in the void with a lightweight substitute. The peanuts make the completed pot lighter and easier to transport. If you just shake the peanuts in the pot without the garbage bag, make sure to use the truly peanut-shaped little noodles (not the concave or hollow ones, which will actually retain water and possibly rot the roots of the plant).

MOIST SOIL MEDIUM

Upon opening the bag of potting mix, check it to see if it is dry. If so, pour some warm water in the package and knead the water into the medium. It may take a while for it to absorb. If you are using a large quantity, pour the soil into a wheelbarrow or onto a plastic drop cloth and add water, mixing until the soil feels moist but not soggy.

AMENDMENTS

If the container will be in a sunny location, you'll need to water it often. Each time you water, soil nutrients are flushed from the soil, so you'll need to fertilize more frequently. One way around this is to purchase a soil mix with water-retentive polymers and slow-release fertilizer, or add these elements yourself. Both can be purchased at the garden center. The water-saving gel, a popular water-retentive polymer, looks like ice cream salt but swells up when it comes in contact with moisture, then slowly releases the water. A small handful of this mixed into a large container of soil is all you need. A long-lasting fertilizer works to ensure continuous plant feeding for up to nine months. These are optional additives, but with my busy schedule, I find they allow me more flexibility between times when I need to water and fertilize my containers.

1.

2.

3.

4.

5.

{Planting a Standard Pot}

When it comes to the technique for planting each container type,
here are the guidelines to follow:

1. Cover the drainage hole with a piece of window screen.
2. Another technique is to cover the bottom with shards of broken
clay pots.
3. Fill the container with a good-quality container mix so that when
the tallest plant is placed inside, the soil line of that plant is about 1 inch
below the rim of the pot.
4. Tuck in the midlevel plants to fill in around the tallest plant.
5. Position low and trailing plants around the edge of the container.

Water thoroughly, avoiding blossoms and leaves. Add more soil if set-
tling occurs.

• Look for specially made brackets to securely attach your window box to a porch railing or wall, or beneath a window. Choose a style to complement your home's décor.

• Make sure the brackets are anchored into solid supports. Once a window box is full of soil, plants, and water, it can become quite heavy.

{ Planting a Window Box }

Window boxes add instant charm to any house. Typically, the boxes are attached below windows, but they can also be defined as any container with a long rectangular shape, such as planters that line the perimeter of a patio.

FOR A CLASSIC WINDOW BOX

Buy or build a box that extends to the edges of the window frame. If you will be planting annuals, the plants tend to be shallow rooted, so any box six inches deep will give them enough room to spread their roots. Other plants may require deeper, heavier boxes. A wooden box benefits from a protective coat of paint or wood preservative. Decay-resistant woods such as redwood, cypress, and cedar are good choices.

1. Make sure the box has drainage holes.

2. Add a plastic liner inside the box to protect it from the effects of wet soil. If you can't find a plastic liner that is the correct size, use a heavyweight garbage bag that has been cut to size. Fill the box with container mix.

3. Slip the largest plant out of the nursery pot and position it in the box. The soil level of the plant should be 1 inch below the top of the box.

4. Plant from the middle out to the ends, staggering the plants.

FOR RECTANGULAR BOX DESIGNS

Determine where the plants will be viewed (whether it will be from one side or both). If they will be seen from just one side, position taller plants in the back and shorter ones in the front. For boxes viewed from both sides, you have a couple of options: line the tallest plants down the middle through the length of the box with shorter plants on either side, or fill one end of the box with the tallest plants and stair-step (tallest to shortest) the remaining plants to the other end.

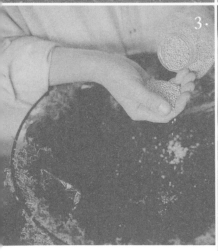

{Hanging Basket}

Overflowing with blooms, flowering baskets are suspended in the air and create a sense of lavish beauty. They are so attention-getting, it is important to choose where you will place them for the best effect. I've hung them along the perimeter or corners of an outdoor area to help define the edges. They are best near sitting areas positioned at a level where they can be most appreciated.

Hanging baskets often dry out quickly, especially if they are in a full-sun location. Daily or sometimes even twice-daily watering is required. The best baskets are covered in blooms, so here are some tips on how to achieve that look.

FOR AN OPEN-WIRE BASKET

1. Soak a package of sphagnum moss in water. Lay pieces of the moss on the wire frame from the inside of the basket and push them through to the outside, overlapping the pieces to create a thick layer.

2. Cut a plastic garbage bag to fit inside the basket, poking several holes in the bottom for drainage. If the planter will be viewed from below, you may choose to fill in the lower area with plants. Cut a small slit through the moss and insert the plants into the sides and bottom. Tuck the moss back into place.

3. Fill the basket with a packaged soil container mix. Check the ingredients listed on the package. If it doesn't contain water-retentive polymers or slow-release fertilizer, mix both into the soil, following package directions.

4. Plant the tallest plants in the center of the basket, surrounded by those that are round and full, with the cascading plants around the circumference so they will trail over the sides. The romance of a hanging basket calls for several of these arching plants.

HANGING BASKET TIPS

• Rest the basket in a bucket or another container for more stability while planting.

• When watering plants located on the sides and bottom of the container, a houseplant watering can with a narrow spout can be used to direct water through the slit directly to the plants' roots.

HAY BASKETS

Semicircular or long half-troughs of heavy black wire with one flat side are called hay baskets. These half-baskets were modeled after the hay baskets found in old barns. They are great for giving a blank wall some color and life.

The planting technique is similar to that of a hanging basket, except that the hay baskets usually come with a coconut palm fiber (coir), sisal (a natural fiber), or a synthetic liner. The material holds in the soil so a garbage-bag liner is not needed. Before you plant the hay basket, mount it securely on the wall. It will be too heavy to move once you fill it with dirt and plants.

With the holder positioned on the wall, place the liner inside the holder and fill it with a basic potting soil. The liner will hold the soil and allow the excess moisture to drain. If you don't like the look of the liner, sphagnum moss can be used to camouflage it. You'll find that if you completely saturate the moss in a bucket of water, it is easier to work with. It will conform to the shape of the basket and also help keep the soil consistently moist.

Now, you are ready for the fun part—filling the container with flowers.

There are several types of clever irrigation systems for containers. For example, a loop of plastic with small holes that emit water surrounds the base of this container. When attached to a hose on a timer, it makes an effective automatic watering system.

CARING FOR CONTAINER PLANTS

WATERING

Consistent watering is critical for the health and vitality of the plants in a container garden. Roots are not able to find water on their own, and you can't rely on rainfall to supply container plants with enough moisture. The soil dries out much faster in a container than it does in the ground.

The frequency that you will need to water your container gardens depends on climate, varieties of plants, the sizes of their root systems, and even the types of containers. As many of us know, midsummer heat can quickly turn a garden oasis into a microdesert. Plants in porous terra-cotta containers are especially susceptible to drying out quickly and may need to be watered two or three times more often than plants in similarly sized plastic containers. In general, the goal is to keep the container soil consistently moist so you never let it get too dry or stay too wet.

When watering your plants, it is important that the water reaches the roots. In order to achieve this, slowly apply water until it begins trickling out the bottom of the container. This can be a bit deceiving if the soil is extremely dry, because the water could run down the sides of the container and straight into the drainage holes, without penetrating the rootball. If you are faced with this condition, slowly water or wet the soil in small, successive doses until you are sure the rootball is saturated. Ideally, the best time to water is early morning. Avoid watering in hot summer sun, as it may scorch the foliage.

If your schedule keeps you on the run, or if you travel often and find it difficult to keep your plants watered regularly, there are several time-saving options that may be of help. You may want to invest in containers that have built-in water reservoirs, where water is held in the lower part of the planter and travels up into the soil as it is needed. Adding water-saving gel to the soil will also prevent the soil from drying out as quickly. When mixed with soil, the crystals act as water place-holders, swelling up as they absorb the water and then slowly releasing moisture. The polymers are especially an advantage when using large thirsty plants in hot dry climates. They are less needed with small plants in cool, cloudy, or wet conditions. If you have several pots on a patio or porch, you can create a mini-irrigation system connected to your outdoor faucet. By adding a timer, your plants will be watered automatically.

Container plants benefit from a regular feeding schedule. Add a slow-release fertilizer to the packaged container mix when you plant (if not already included in the soil) and a dilute solution of water-soluble fertilizer to every other watering.

FERTILIZING

Seasonal plants, especially annual flowers, need more feeding than slower-growing trees and shrubs. Annuals grow quickly, exhausting nutrients in the soil in the process. In general, I follow this program to feed the plants in my containers. I start by mixing about three tablespoons of slow-release fertilizer into each gallon of potting soil (providing it is not already part of the blend), or by just following the instructions on the fertilizer label. After planting the containers, I begin using an all-purpose water-soluble fertilizer (10-10-10), which is ten parts nitrogen, ten parts phosphorus, and ten parts potassium, but I use only one-fourth of the suggested amount. If the container is made up of mostly flowering plants, use a fertilizer with a high phosphorus content (such as 10-27-10). Seaweed extracts and fish fertilizers are good if you prefer organic fertilizers. Use this weakened solution for every other watering or follow the instructions for the specific fertilizer you select.

PEST CARE

As you water and fertilize your containers, it is a good time to give your plants a close inspection to check for signs of pests or disease. Yellowing leaves, lots of dropped or brown-edged foliage, visible pest insects, or telltale signs such as brown specks or sticky drops on the leaves are early warning signs that your plant needs immediate attention. The same techniques used in your garden apply here as well. Quick attention to the problem is important. Remove the affected plants or areas of the plant immediately and discard them. You can handpick or give your plant a quick spray of water to remove visible insects, or use other controls if necessary.

I am more comfortable using organic means first, and applying stronger chemicals only when those methods fail. It is important that the plants be well hydrated and not in direct sunlight as they are being treated for disease problems.

GROOMING

To look their best, container gardens need to be pruned and pinched back. Tending to grooming details promotes healthy foliage, fresh flowers, and clean soil surfaces. Here is a checklist of quick and easy steps to give your containers that well-cared-for look.

1. **Deadhead**—Pinch off or prune spent blossoms as soon as they begin to wilt or fade.

2. **Trim up**—Use scissors or pruners to snip back fast-growing plants that are becoming too aggressive with their container mates. The plants will evolve as they grow. The main idea is to keep the design balanced and appealing, not unruly.

3. **Remove unsightly foliage**—Pinch off any leaves that are yellowing, withered, disfigured, damaged, or otherwise unattractive.

4. **Encourage compact growth**—You can help plants maintain a dense, busy shape by pinching off the growing tip and the first pair or two of leaves on each plant stem. Vines often can become leggy, showing signs of bare stems. Trimming them back often stimulates new growth and a fuller appearance.

5. **Remove weeds**—Unwelcome plants can occasionally pop up. Remove them as they appear.

6. **Mulch**—By applying a layer of compost, shredded bark, or pebbles to the soil surface, you can slow down water loss and add an attractive finishing touch to the

appearance of your planter. It works best for single-plant containers such as shrubs, trees, or other plants where the soil surface is clearly visible.

SLIP-INS

Some plants, such as perennials and spring-flowering bulbs, flower once and then will not make much more of a contribution to the overall design of the container. When this happens, simply remove the plant with a hand trowel and either transplant it to a flowerbed or discard it. Slip in a replacement to fill in the gap, keeping the container looking fresh and new.

OVERWINTERING CONTAINERS

As temperatures drop, plants and pots suffer the effects. Terra-cotta containers and any others with porous surfaces can chip, crack, or otherwise become damaged as water freezes and expands on their surfaces. Here are some winter survival tips that can help.

1. As you prepare for cold weather, take an inventory of your containers and decide which plants you want to save and which you will discard.

2. In some cases, you may want to move the entire pot indoors to overwinter. Otherwise, you'll need to divide and transplant the plants according to how they will be kept. Some can take low light, dry air, and the warmth of indoor rooms, while others do better on sunny porches that are kept above freezing.

3. Transplant perennials suited for your zone into flower-beds, or if you don't have room, share them with friends or other fellow gardeners who do. Transplant them early enough in the season so the plants have a chance to settle in and grow some roots before the soil freezes.

4. Once all porous surface containers or those that are not frostproof have been emptied, clean them thoroughly and store them out of the cold weather.

5. Outdoor container plants can handle freezing temperatures much better if the soil is kept moist. It insulates the roots far better than dry soil.

6. Remove saucers and other drip trays from underneath outdoor containers where water may collect and freeze, damaging the pot.

7. Outdoor containers benefit when placed directly on soil surfaces rather than wood or concrete. The soil offers radiant heat and insulation. If possible, sink the container into the ground and surround it with a heavy layer of mulch. Choose sheltered locations out of the wind.

8. For heavy outdoor containers that cannot be moved indoors, protect exposed surfaces with a layered approach. Cover the surface with bubble wrap, followed by a weatherproof tarp and a final, more attractive covering of burlap or other material. Another method is to create a chicken-wire cage a foot taller than the plants and six inches wider on all sides, going around the pot. Fill in the area between the walls and wire with mulch, straw, or fallen leaves.

9. As a preventive measure, you can also apply water seal to the outer surfaces and top rims of porous containers. This keeps water from penetrating and damaging the pots.

To keep containers looking their best, remove spent blooms and prune unruly or damaged vegetation during the growing season.

Plant Directory

PLANT CULTURAL INFORMATION

'ACCENT CORAL' IMPATIENS
(*Impatiens walleriana* 'Accent Coral') Annual, 12″ tall, 8–12″ wide, shade to partial shade. Large coral-pink flowers that bloom from May to frost.

'ACCENT DEEP PINK' IMPATIENS
(*Impatiens walleriana* 'Accent Deep Pink') Annual, 12″ tall, 8–12″ wide, shade to partial shade. Large deep pink flowers that bloom from May to frost.

ANNUAL PINK DIANTHUS
(*Dianthus chinensis*) Annual, size varies with variety, full sun. Fragrant blooms appear all summer. Good for spring and fall gardens as well. Prefers well-drained soil.

'ANTIQUE ROSE' NEMESIA
(*Nemesia caerulea* hybrid 'Antique Rose') Annual, 10″ tall, 9″ wide, sun to partial shade. Cultivar of South African native with 1–3″-long spatulalike leaves and ½–1″-wide 2-tone pink fragrant flowers with yellow throats that bloom in terminal clusters. Best in cool temperatures of spring and fall.

'AUGUST MOON' HOSTA
(*Hosta* 'August Moon') Perennial (Z 3–9), 20–24″ tall, 36–42″ wide, morning sun with afternoon shade. Foliage plant with large, heart-shaped leaves and prominent veins. Attractive puckering and some crinkling. Gold color glows on overcast days and at dusk. Near white, bell-shaped flowers borne on scapes 24–26″ tall, 35–40 flowers per scape.

AUTUMN FERN
(*Dryopteris erythrosora*) Perennial (Z 6–9), 18–24″ tall, 16″ wide, shade. Dwarf-growing fern, young papery fronds display coppery red color maturing deep green and deeply cut. Spreads by underground stems.

'BARBARA' PROPHET SERIES CHRYSANTHEMUM
(*Chrysanthemum* × *morifolium* 'Barbara') Perennial (Z 4–9), 1–2′ tall, 18″–2′ wide, sun. Showy, with bright purple small pompon-type flowers. Blooms in mid-September and has good color retention.

BATFACE CUPHEA
(*Cuphea llavea*) Perennial (Z 10–12), 24″ tall, 30″ wide, sun. Bushy subshrub, bright green oval pointed leaves, thin, orange-red tubular flowers, tipped white, touch of black, aka cigar flower, fire cracker plant.

'BATH'S PINK' DIANTHUS
(*Dianthus gratianopolitanus* 'Bath's Pink') Perennial (Z 4–8), 6–8″ tall, full sun. Soft pink, fragrant flowers rise above mat-forming glaucous foliage. Evergreen. Prefers well-drained soil. Blooms April–June.

BELL FLOWER HESPERALOË
(*Hesperaloë campanulata*) Perennial (Z 8–12) 3′ tall, 3′ wide, sun. Spiky accent plant with stiff, ½″ wide, lime green leaves, with white fibers along the margins. In the summer it sends up a tall spike of light pink flowers that attract hummingbirds. Drought tolerant once established.

'BETH' PROPHET SERIES CHRYSANTHEMUM
(*Chrysanthemum* × *morifolium* 'Beth') Perennial (Z 4–9), 1–2′ high, 18–26″ wide, sun. Bold purple cushion flowers averaging 2 inches in diameter comprised almost entirely of ray petals. Slightly crested in appearance. Ideal round habit that blooms in mid-September.

'BEWITCHED' DIANTHUS
(*Dianthus gratianopolitanus* 'Bewitched') Perennial (Z4–8), 8–12″ tall, full sun. Light pink flower with magenta ring. Excellent performer even in very hot climates. Prefers well-drained soil. Exceptionally long flowering period.

'BLACK AND BLUE' SALVIA
(*Salvia guaranitica* 'Black and Blue') Perennial (Z 7–10), 4–6′ tall, 2–3′ wide, sun to partial shade. Opposite ovate 4–6″ long leaves on tall spikes with numerous sky blue snapdragonlike flowers emerging from black calyxes. Blooms prolifically early summer through fall.

'BLACK MAGIC' ELEPHANT'S EAR
(*Colocasia esculenta* 'Black Magic') Perennial (Z 9–12), 3–6′ tall, 3–6′ wide, sun, distinctive purplish black arrow-shaped black leaves (up to 2 feet) with sturdy stems supporting them from below, grown from a tuber.

'BLACKIE' SWEET POTATO VINE
(*Ipomoea batatas* 'Blackie') Perennial (Z 9–12), 10′ tall, 10′ wide, sun. Ornamental sweet potato vine with purple-black foliage, heart-shaped leaves.

BLOODY SORREL
(*Rumex sanguineus*) Perennial (Z 6–10), 36–40″ tall, 10 –12″ wide, sun. Dark stems, lance-shaped leaves that grow to 6" long with red veins, panicles of tiny green flowers in early to midsummer.

BLUE HYACINTH
(*Hyacinthus orientalis*) Perennial bulb (Z 5–9) 4–8″ tall, 2–6″ wide, partial shade to shade. Blue flowers densely packed 6–30 per stem in spring, linear leaves, dark green.

'BLUE MOON' TORENIA
(*Torenia fournieri* hybrid 'Blue Moon') Annual, 12–15″ tall, 10″ wide, sun to shade. Bold-colored blue flowers with a trailing habit. Loves heat and full sun. Ideal for the humid South.

'BLUE SHADES' COLUMBINE
(*Aquilegia* hybrids 'Blue Shades') Perennial (Z 3–9) 24–30″ tall, 24–36″ wide, shade to partial shade. Delicate long-spurred flowers in shades of light blue that bloom in early summer. Prefers shade when temperatures get hot. Rich soil.

'BLUE SHOWERS' BACOPA
(*Sutera Cordata* 'Blue Showers') Annual/Tender perennial (Z 9–10), 3″ tall, 12″-wide vine, partial sun to shade. Trailing vines with bright true blue flowers brighten mixed containers, showy baskets, and pots. Well-branched stems, spreading habit, and vigorous growth add to the appeal. Flowers continuously from spring through fall.

'BLUE STAR' JUNIPER
(*Juniperus squamata* 'Blue Star') Perennial (Z 4–8), 2–3′ tall, 3–4′ wide, full sun. Evergreen with very blue foliage, on dense spreading and mounding branches. Creates a colorful contrast. Evergreen. Slow grower.

'BLUEBERRY SACHET' NEMESIA
(*Nemesia* × *hybrida* 'Blueberry Sachet') Annual/Tender perennial 16–18″ tall, 10–12″ wide, sun to partial shade. Early-flowering deep blue–purple flowers on a compact plant. Keep consistently moist, prefers cooler temperatures.

'BRANDYWINE' FOAM FLOWER
(*Tiarella cordifolia* 'Brandywine') Perennial (Z 3–9), 12″ tall, 16–20″ wide, partial shade to full shade. Spreads by underground stems, airy sprays of tiny, wine-colored flowers on fine stems. Hairy, lobed, toothed, heart-shaped leaves up to 4′ long.

'BRAVO' GERANIUM
(*Pelargonium* × *hortorum* 'Bravo') Tender perennial (Z 9–11), 12–14″ tall, 10–12″ wide, morning sun, afternoon shade. Dark pink semidouble medium-height geranium, heat tolerant.

'BRIGHTSIDE' SUNSCAPE DAISY
(*Osteospermum* 'Brightside') Perennial (Z 10–11), 10–12″ tall, 10″ wide full sun. Clear, bright white 2–3″ daisies with a blue eye. Uniform plants bloom until the weather gets too hot in August but perk up again in the cool fall.

'BRONZE BEAUTY' AJUGA
(*Ajuga reptans* 'Bronze Beauty') Perennial (Z 3–10), 5″ tall, 6–8″ wide, partial sun. Low, carpet-forming plant that spreads by runners. Bronze leaves and blue flowers. Useful for edging, or ground cover in shady areas or beneath larger shrubs.

'BUNNY BLUE' SEDGE
(*Carex laxiculmis* 'Bunny Blue') Perennial (Z 7–10), 10–12″ tall, 12–18″ wide, sun. Well-mannered and low-growing grasslike plant with wide blue-green leaves. A wonderful foil for hot colors; thrives on neglect.

'BUTTERFLY BLUE' SCABIOSA
(*Scabiosa columbaria* 'Butterfly Blue') Perennial (Z 4–8), foliage only 6–8″ tall, flowers 12–15″ tall, 12″ wide, full sun. Nearly flat gray-green basal foliage hugs the ground. Lacy lavender-blue, 2″ flowers bloom on slender 12–15″ stems from late spring through early fall.

CABBAGE
(*Brassica oleracea*) Annual (Z 1–11), 8–10″ tall, 8–10″ wide, full sun. Used as young seedlings in containers primarily for the blue-gray leaf color. Can be left to grow to maturity, depending on the composition, or transplanted into the garden to form a solid head. Can take light frosts without damage.

'CALLIE IVORY II' CALIBRACHOA
(*Calibrachoa* hybrid 'Callie Ivory II') Annual, 8″ tall, 20″ wide, sun. Plant form and flower shapes reminiscent of small petunias. Trailing habit. Well-branched plants produce masses of blooms in soft ivory.

'CARITA DEEP PINK' ANGELONIA
(*Angelonia angustifolia* 'Carita Deep Pink') Annual, 18″ tall, 24″ wide, sun. Summer snapdragons with a bushy, branching habit and deep pink, miniature orchid-like blooms

'CARITA PURPLE' ANGELONIA
(*Angelonia angustifolia* 'Carita Purple') Annual, 18″ tall, 24″ wide, sun. Summer snapdragons with a bushy, branching habit and purple miniature orchidlike blooms.

'CARLOS' LANTANA
(*Lantana camara* 'Carlos') Tender perennial (Z 10–11), 12–24″ tall, 24–36″ wide, full sun. Tropical-appearing shrub with a mounding habit. Showy clusters of red-purple, orange, and gold-centered flowers that bloom through the season. Thrives in sun and heat. Attracts butterflies and hummingbirds.

'CASCADIAS IMPROVED CHARLIE' PETUNIA
(*Petunia hybrida* 'Cascadias Improved Charlie' Annual, 8″ tall, 12–18″ wide, full sun to partial shade. Petunia hybrid with velvety blue-purple flowers. Performs well in warm temperatures. Summer annual in most parts of the country, may overwinter in areas with very mild winter temperatures.

'CHAMELEON' EUPHORBIA
(*Euphorbia dulcis* 'Chameleon') Perennial (Z 5–9), 12–18″ tall, 12–18″ wide, sun to partial shade. Herbaceous perennial with deep bronzy purple foliage set with golden blooms in late spring to early summer. Drought tolerant. Parts of plant are poisonous if ingested. Milky sap may cause skin irritation.

CHINESE WILD GINGER
(*Asarum splendens*) Perennial (Z 6–8), 5–8″ tall, 5–8″ wide, shade to partial shade. Vigorous Chinese ginger with large, dark green pointed leaves elegantly mottled with silver. In early spring 2" dark purple flowers bloom underneath the large leaves, at the soil level.

CHIVES
(*Allium schoenoprasum*) Perennial (Z 3–9), 12–18″ tall, 6–9″ wide, full sun. Bulbous herb with clumps of grasslike, bright green, upright, cylindrical, hollow leaves with a distinctive onion smell. Bears tiny, purple or white, bell-shaped flowers tightly packed into a rounded head that blooms from May to July.

'CHOCOLATE' WHITE SNAKEROOT
(*Eupatorium rugosum* 'Chocolate') Perennial (Z 4–8), 3–4′ tall, 3–4′ wide, tolerates full sun but prefers partial shade. Rich chocolate-tinted foliage with purple stems and clusters of white flowers that appear in late summer to early fall. Foliage color is reduced in intense sun/heat. Habit is rounded.

'COMET PINK' ARGYRANTHEMUM
(*Argyranthemum frutescens* 'Comet Pink') Annual, 16–20″ tall, 10–12″ wide, full sun. A good season extender that flowers from spring through early summer. Upright habit with light pink, daisy-shaped blooms with a yellow eye.

'CONCORD GRAPE' SPIDERWORT
(*Tradescantia* × *andersoniana* 'Concord Grape') Perennial (Z 4–9), 2′ tall, 12–15″ wide, sun to partial shade. Upright habit with purplish blue flowers borne in clusters. Prefers moist but well-drained soils.

COPPER PLANT
(*Acalypha godseffiana* 'Heterophylla') Annual, 8–16″ tall, sun to partial shade. Tropical shrub, bushy habit with multi-colored leaves festooned in green, pink and bronze, and cream. Low drought tolerance, wilts easily.

'CROWN WHITE' PANSY
(*Viola* × *wittrockiana* 'Crown White') Annual, 6–8″ tall, 5–8″ wide, full sun. A cool-season favorite for the spring and fall garden, clear white face with a yellow eye.

CURLY YUCCA
(*Beschorneria tubiflora*) Tender perennial (Z 10–12), 3′ tall, 26″ wide, sun. Mexican native related to the agave and yucca, this perennial succulent has a compact rosette of slender straplike green leaves that are curled. This is a new variety that may be difficult to find.

DARK PINK ENGLISH DAISY
(*Bellis perennis*) Biennial (Z 4–8), 5″ tall, full sun to partial shade. Big fluffy dark pink blooms over compact mounds of green foliage.

'DEBONAIR' CHRYSANTHEMUM
(*Chrysanthemum* × *morifolium* 'Debonair') Perennial (Z 4–9), 1–2′ high, 18–26″ wide, sun. Strong, spreading plants with medium-size dark lavender flowers. Excellent flower durability and color retention. Flowers average 2″ in diameter comprised of ray petals. Blooms in mid-September.

DINOSAUR KALE
(*Brassica oleracea* 'Lacinato') Annual, 24–36″ tall, 18–24″ wide, full sun. Gray-green, highly textured foliage persists even after the first frost.

'DUCHESS DEEP BLUE' TORENIA
(*Torenia fournieri* 'Duchess Deep Blue') Annual, 6–8″ high, 6–8″ wide, full sun to partial shade. Wishbone flower, tight mounding habit with a profusion of dark indigo, pitcher-shaped blooms marked with a yellow throat.

'DUCHESS LIGHT BLUE' TORENIA
(*Torenia fournieri* 'Duchess Light Blue') Annual, 6–8″ high, 6–8″ wide, full sun to partial shade. Wishbone flower, tight mounding habit with a profusion of light blue and white pitcher-shaped blooms marked with a yellow throat.

DUSTY MILLER
(*Centaurea cineraria*) Annual, 6–12″ tall, 9–12″ wide, full sun to partial shade. Glaucous, deeply cut, upright foliage with a velvety texture. Drought tolerant.

DWARF ALBERTA SPRUCE
(*Picea glauca* 'Conica') Evergreen shrub (Z 3–6), 6–20′ tall, 3–8′ wide, full sun. Compact, cone-shaped evergreen shrub with very fine, dense light green needle-type foliage. Prefers moist but well-drained soil.

'EMPEROR' FLOWERING KALE
(*Brassica oleracea* 'Emperor') Annual, 6" high, 8–12" wide, full sun. Heavily fringed uniform leaves persist even after the first frost.

ENGLISH IVY
(*Hedera helix*) Perennial (Z 5–10), 12–18" tall, full sun to full shade. Evergreen, arrow-shaped leaves, trailing habit. Prefers some shade in Z 7–10. Well-drained soil.

'EVERGOLD' SEDGE
(*Carex hachijoensis* 'Evergold') Perennial (Z 6–9), 12" tall, 14" wide, partial shade. Evergreen, grasslike, creamy yellow and green foliage. Mounding habit. Tolerates both moist and dry soil.

EYEBALL PLANT
(*Spilanthes acmella*) Annual, 12–18" tall, 12–15" wide, full sun to partial shade. Unique, petal-less blooms are gold with a red center resembling an eye. Blooms from midsummer through fall.

'FELICIA' CHRYSANTHEMUM
(*Chrysanthemum* × *morifolium* 'Felicia') Perennial (Z 4–9), 1–2' high, 18–26" wide, sun. Blooms early September in lavender daisy-type flowers with gold centers. Uniquely shaped dark-green foliage.

FERN-LEAF LAVENDER
(*Lavandula pinnata*) Tender perennial (Z 9–10), 2–3' tall, 2–3' wide, full sun. Deeply cut, fernlike leaves with tall flower stalks bearing spikes of deep purple flowers in summer. Will not survive temperatures below 32 degrees Fahrenheit.

**'FIREFLY IMPROVED SALMON'
MINI IMPATIENS**
(*Impatiens walleriana* 'Firefly Improved Salmon') Annual, 6–8" tall, 8–10" wide, shade to partial shade. A charming mini-impatiens, with dainty salmon ½-inch-wide flowers.

'FIREFLY LIGHT SALMON' MINI IMPATIENS
(*Impatiens walleriana* 'Firefly Light Salmon') Annual, 6–8" tall, 8–10" wide, shade to partial shade. A charming mini-impatiens, with dainty ½-inch-wide flowers in light salmon.

'FIREWORKS' GOLDENROD
(*Solidago rugosa* 'Fireworks') Perennial (Z 5–9), 3½ tall, 2½–3' wide, full sun. Gracefully arching spires of yellow flowers resemble fireworks. Blooms in late summer or early fall.

FIVE COLOR FALSE HOLLY
(*Osmanthus heterophyllus* 'Goshiki') Perennial (Z 6–9), 3½' high, 3–5' wide, filtered sun to partial shade. Evergreen shrub with compact mounding habit. New leaves are tinged with pink, maturing to creamy yellow and splotched dark green. Fragrant blooms appear in fall.

'FLAVIRAMEA' YELLOW TWIG DOGWOOD
(*Cornus sericea* 'Flaviramea') Perennial (Z 3–8), 6' high, 12' wide, full sun to partial shade. Deciduous shrub with striking bright yellow-green winter stems. Prefers moist soil.

'FLORAL SHOWERS FUCHSIA' SNAPDRAGON
(*Antirrhinum majus* 'Floral Showers Fuchsia') Annual, 6–10" high, partial shade. Upright stems bear clusters of hot pink pealike blooms. Ideal for the cool months of the growing season.

'FLORIDA SWEETHEART' CALADIUM
(*Caladium* 'Florida Sweetheart') Tender perennial (Z 9–11), 12–18" tall, 6–9" wide, partial to full shade. Rose leaves with darker rose veins, highlighted by a soft green edge. More sun tolerant than most caladiums.

'FOXY NATASHA' EUROPEAN PROPHET SERIES CHRYSANTHEMUM
(*Chrysanthemum* × *morifolium* 'Foxy Natasha') Perennial (Z 4–9), 1–2' high, 18–26" wide, sun. Dark red ray petals surrounding a light green daisy eye that matures to yellow. One of the earliest of garden mums to flower and adaptable to most any size container.

'FREESTYLE LAVENDER' IVY GERANIUM
(*Pelargonium* × *peltatum* 'Freestyle Lavender') Annual, 12–14" tall, 12–14" wide, partial shade. Free-flowering, semi-double flowers cover the plant. Compact, trailing habit with semisucculent foliage and stems. Prefers evenly moist soil.

'FROSTY MORN' SEDUM
(*Sedum erythrostictum* 'Frosty Morn') Perennial (Z 3–9), 12" tall, 12" wide, full sun. Succulent, pale green leaves are edged in white. Pale pink blooms appear August–September. Low maintenance and drought tolerant.

GANGES PRIMROSE
(*Asystasia gangetica*) Perennial (Z 11–12), 2' tall, 2' wide, partial shade. Evergreen soft-wooded scrambling shrub, stems root on contact with ground, bright green leaves, broad, round. Flowers cream to rose-purple in summer.

'GENERAL SIKORSKY' CLEMATIS
(*Clematis* 'General Sikorsky') Perennial (Z 4–9), 8–12′ tall, 3–10′ wide, full sun to partial shade. This profuse bloomer produces huge 6–8″ in diameter, dark lavender flowers with a tint of red in the center. Blooms June–September.

'GLACIER' ENGLISH IVY
(*Hedera helix* 'Glacier') Perennial (Z 5–10), 6–8″ tall, 12–18″ wide, full sun to full shade. Evergreen, silver-gray variegated, arrow-shaped leaves, trailing habit. Prefers some shade in Z 7–10. Well-drained soil.

'GNOME PINK' DWARF GLOBE AMARANTH
(*Gomphrena* 'Gnome Pink') Annual, 6″ tall, 6″ wide, sun. Compact habit. Flowers profusely all season with round, cloverlike blooms. Nice dried flower. Good for hot, dry conditions.

'GOLDEN BABY' IVY
(*Hedera helix* 'Golden Baby') Perennial (Z 5–10), 12–18″ tall, full sun to full shade. Evergreen, arrow-shaped leaves with broad yellow margins, trailing habit. Prefers some shade in Z 7–10. Well-drained soil.

GOLDEN CREEPING JENNY
(*Lysimachia nummularia* 'Aurea') Perennial (Z 3–8), 3″ tall, 10–12″ wide, full sun to light shade. Trailing habit with dime-sized golden leaves that cover the stems. Prefers moist soil.

'GORDEN COOPER' PINK TULIP
(*Tulipa* 'Gorden Cooper') Bulb, 12-14″ tall, 8–10″ wide, full sun. Medium to pale pink cup-shaped flowers. Purchase bulbs in the fall for spring blooms.

'GRACE' PROPHET SERIES CHRYSANTHEMUM
(*Chrysanthemum* × *morifolium* 'Grace') Perennial (Z 4–9), 1–2′ high, 18–26″ wide, sun. Orange-bronze daisy-type blooms display a slight halo encircling the daisy eye. Rounded, almost ball-like growth habit. Flowers in mid-September.

GREAT BLUE LOBELIA
(*Lobelia siphilitica*) Perennial (Z 5–9), 1–4′ tall, 12″ wide, full sun to partial shade. Purple-blue spires of blooms appear July–September. Prefers moist soil. Good hummingbird plant.

'HAMELN' DWARF FOUNTAIN GRASS
(*Pennisetum alopecuroides* 'Hameln') Perennial (Z 6–9), 2–5′ tall, 2–4′ wide, full sun. Clump-forming, evergreen grass with mid- to dark-green leaves. Prefers well-drained soil. Cut back dead top growth in early spring.

'HARBOUR DWARF' NANDINA
(*Nandina domestica* 'Harbour Dwarf') Perennial (Z 6–9), 18″ tall, 2½ wide, full sun to partial shade. Round, compact shrub with evergreen foliage that is beautiful in fall and winter, turning orange-red to bronzy-red in color. Heat tolerant.

'HELENE VON STEIN' LAMB'S EAR
(*Stachys byzantina* 'Helene Von Stein') Perennial (Z 4–10), 8–10″ tall, 10–12″ wide, sun to partial shade. Wooly soft gray broad leaves that are twice the size of any other lamb's ear variety; a strong grower with a clump-forming habit and small purple flowers borne on upright stalks.

HEN AND CHICKS
(*Sempervivum* hybrids) Perennial (Z 3–8), 3″ tall, 4″ wide, spreading, full sun. Mat-forming succulent, waxy, dark green rosettes of fleshy leaves forming smaller rosettes or "chicks" as it grows. Great for rock gardens, walls, or borders, in dry, well-drained soil.

'HERMANN'S PRIDE' LAMIASTRUM
(*Lamiastrum galeobdolon* 'Hermann's Pride') Perennial (Z 3–10) 10″ tall, 36″ wide, shade. Spreading stoloniferous perennial. Dense clusters of yellow flowers in spring. Striking silvery markings on foliage. Likes well-drained soil.

'HIGHSIDE' SUNSCAPE DAISY
(*Osteospermum fruticosum* 'Highside') Annual, 12″ high, 18″ wide, full sun. South African origin, white daisylike flower with blue eye grows best in a well-drained soil and in full sun. In southern climates, excessive humidity may be a problem.

'HILO BEAUTY' ALOCASIA
(*Alocasia* 'Hilo Beauty') Perennial (Z 8–10), 24–36″ tall, 24–36″ wide, semishade. Beautifully marked large heart-shaped leaves sport a camouflage pattern of dark and light shades of yellows and greens. Keep consistently moist. Lift and store tubers over winter in northern climates

'HOOSIER HARMONY' HOSTA
(*Hosta* 'Hoosier Harmony' Perennial (Z 4–8), 24″ tall, 36″ wide, semi to full shade. Rapid growth rate forms a large mound. Leaves have gold centers edged with an apple green margin. Pure white fragrant flowers in midsummer.

'HUSKERS RED' PENSTEMON
(*Penstemon digitalis* 'Huskers Red') Perennial (Z 3– 8), 36″ tall, 24″ wide, sun. Rich bronze-red foliage accents the 30″-tall plants, providing a rich contrast to the striking masses of white, airy flower stalks.

'ICE FOLLIES' DAFFODIL
(*Narcissus* sp.) Perennial bulb, (Z 3–9), 12–18″ tall, 6–9″ wide, sun to partial shade. Early-blooming daffodil with icy white petals with a cream trumpet. A reliable performer that produces year after year.

'IMPERIAL BLUE' PLUMBAGO
(*Plumbago auriculata* 'Imperial Blue') Tender perennial (Z 8–11), 36–48″ tall, 36–48″ wide, full sun to partial shade. Phloxlike clusters of light to medium blue flowers that are prolific during the warmer months of the year. Long, arching branches hold handsome medium green leaves.

'INA MAE' BEGONIA
(*Begonia × Ina Mae*) Annual, 30–36″ tall, 18–24″ wide, shade to partial shade. Giant angel-wing beauty with bronze-colored foliage and clusters of pendulous pink flowers.

'INGELISE' VARIEGATED IVY
(*Hedera helix* 'Ingelise') Perennial (Z 6–10), 6–12″ tall, 1–3′ wide, sun to shade. Ivy vine with small green leaves (similar to 'Needlepoint') with pale green and cream variegation.

JAPANESE PAINTED FERN
(*Athyrium niponicum* var. 'Pictum') Perennial (Z 3–8), 12–15″ tall, 18″ wide, full to partial shade. Olive green fronds with metallic silver sheen, red stems. Thrives in light shade, with moist conditions.

'KEWENSIS' TRAILING EUONYMUS
(*Euonymus fortunei* 'Kewensis') Perennial (Z 4–8), 1–3″ tall, 1–3′ wide, sun to partial shade. Very low-growing, prostrate, trailing ground cover with dainty, rounded evergreen leaves that spreads along the ground, rooting as it goes, until it reaches a vertical surface, which it may begin to climb.

'KIMBERLY QUEEN' FERN
(*Nephrolepis* hybrids) Tender perennial (Z 8–10), 2–3′ tall, 2–3′ wide, bright filtered light to shade. Popular upright Boston-looking fern, also known as Australian sword fern. Becoming popular in United States as it can handle more sun and rain than the Boston fern.

'KOPPER KING' HIBISCUS
(*Hibiscus moscheutos* 'Kopper King') Perennial (Z 4–9), 3–4′ tall, 3–4′ wide, sun. Enormous, open-faced pinkish white flowers with deep red eyes that spread 8 to 12 inches in diameter. Deeper color spreads out along the veins, adding subtle radiating pinstripes to the petals. Flowers are set off by richly colored reddish purple foliage.

LADY FERN
(*Athyrium filix-femina*) Perennial (Z 3–8), 24–48″ tall, 24–48″ wide, partial sun to light shade. Lady Fern is a graceful, cold hardy fern native to much of the northern hemisphere. One hundred eighty species available, most with cut, light green lacy fronds.

'LADY IN RED' SALVIA
(*Salvia coccinea* 'Lady in Red') Annual, 1½–2½′ tall, 1½–2′ wide, sun to partial shade. Seed-grown South American native with ovate, translucent, 1–2″-long leaves and whorled scarlet flowers on numerous racemes. Blooms summer through fall.

'LA MARNE' ROSE
(*Rosa* 'La Marne') Perennial (Z 5–9), 4–5′ tall, 3–5′ wide, sun. Shrub polyantha rose almost always covered with clusters of delicate pink cupped flowers brightened by white centers. Few thorns and disease-resistant foliage.

LAMB'S EAR
(*Stachys byzantina*) Perennial (Z 4–10), 6–12″ tall, 12–15″ wide, sun to partial shade. Grown primarily for its soft gray, woolly lamb's ear-shaped foliage. Leafy flower spikes with lilac blossoms are attractive to bees and hummingbirds. Self-seeds freely.

'LANAI ROYAL PURPLE' VERBENA
(*Verbena hybrida* 'Lanai Royal Purple') Annual, 10–12″ tall, 2–3′ wide, sun. Sprawling habit covered with true violet-purple flowers. Especially mildew resistant as well as heat tolerant.

'LASER PINK FLAME' CYCLAMEN
(*Cyclamen persicum intermediat* 'Laser Pink Flame') Annual, 5–12″ tall, 5–12″ wide, shade. Hybrid of Mediterranean native used most often as a houseplant. Prolific upright blooms with swept-back petals and heart-shaped silver marbled leaves. Needs bright indirect light and cool temperatures 55–70 degrees F.

'LASER SALMON' CYCLAMEN
(*Cyclamen persicum intermediat* 'Laser Salmon') Annual, 5–12″ tall, 5–12″ wide, shade. Hybrid of Mediterranean native used most often as a houseplant. Prolific upright blooms with swept-back petals and heart-shaped silver marbled leaves. Needs bright indirect light and cool temperatures 55–70 degrees F.

LAVENDER CLEMATIS
(*Clematis*) Perennial (Z 3–8), 10–12′ tall, 30′ wide, sun to partial shade. Long-blooming 6 to 8″ lavender-blue flowers. Foliage enjoys sun while the roots like cool, moist conditions. Find a lavender variety suited for your area.

LAVENDER COTTON

(*Santolina chamaecyparissus*) Perennial (Z 6–9), 12–18" tall, 9–12" wide, full sun. Evergreen shrub has fragrant, narrow, and crinkled silvery gray leaves on mound-shaped plants. Drought resistant. Can be clipped.

LAVENDER CREEPING THRIFT

(*Phlox subulata*) Perennial (Z 3–8), 3–6" tall, 18–24" wide, sun. Spectacular when it flowers in lavender blooms in spring, forming a dense carpet of color. This species thrives in full sun in almost any well-drained soil. Little maintenance is needed. After flowers fade in spring, a mat of needlelike ½–¼"-thick foliage persists. Drought resistant.

LAVENDER PENTAS

(*Pentas lanceolata*) Annual, 12–36" tall, 24" wide, full sun. Dark green, lance-shaped, somewhat furry and deeply veined leaves provide a lush backdrop for prolific clusters of starlike five-petaled lavender flowers that appear spring through autumn. Blooms are held in terminal clusters and self-deadhead and are attractive to butterflies.

'LEILANI BLUE' AGERATUM

(*Ageratum houstonianum* 'Leilani Blue') Annual, 14–16" tall, 10–12" wide, sun to partial shade. Large, clear, sky-blue powder puff-shaped flowers on compact, well-branched plants with dark green foliage. Blooms from May to frost.

'LEMON CHIFFON SORBET' VIOLA

(*Viola cornuta* 'Lemon Chiffon Sorbet') Annual, 8–12" tall, 6–8" wide, sun to partial shade. Cool-season flowers can freeze solid and revive. Also thrives in low light conditions better than pansies. Creamy yellow color.

LIGHT PINK ENGLISH DAISY

(*Bellis perennis*) Perennial (Z 4–10), 6–10" tall, 6–9" wide, sun to partial shade. Wonderfully compact plant with light pink daisy flowers that bloom all summer. It self-seeds readily, so be prepared to thin your beds or keep bellis in an area where it may spread freely.

'LIMELIGHT' LICORICE PLANT

(*Helichrysum petiolare* 'Limelight') Tender perennial (Z 8–10), 12–18" tall, 24–36" wide, morning sun to partial shade. Light green to chartreuse foliage may bleach in all-day sun. Thrives in average to dry soil (they require even moisture in the South and the West). Prune if sprawling stems reach beyond their allotted space.

'LITTLE WHITE PET' ROSE

Perennial (Zone 5–9), 1–3' tall, 2' wide, sun. Small compact polyantha shrub rose with white 1" blossoms, pink-tinged buds. Profuse clusters of blooms from June through hard frost, very hardy. Foliage is small, dark green, and semi-glossy.

'MAGNUS' CONEFLOWER

(*Echinacea purpurea* 'Magnus') Perennial (Z 3–9), 2–4' tall, 2' wide, sun. U.S. native with dark green leaves and solitary, daisylike flower heads. Drought tolerant and requires well-drained soil. 'Magnus' has larger, more horizontal flowers (approximately 7" wide) of deeper purple than other varieties.

MAIDENHAIR FERN

(*Adiantum pedatum*) Perennial (Z 4–9), 8–18" tall, 10–18" wide, partial to full shade. Finely textured, frilly fronds. Used as a houseplant as well as in the garden. Deciduous, clump-forming fern that prefers rich, damp, shady locations.

'MARGARITA PINK' MOSS ROSE

(*Portulaca grandiflora* 'Margarita Pink') Annual, 4–6" tall, 12" wide, sun. Portulaca are drought-tolerant South American natives that thrive with hot conditions and low nutrition. 'Margarita Pink' has a mounded habit and semi-double, pink 1½" flowers.

MARGARITAVILLE YUCCA

(*Yucca recurvifolia* 'Hinvargus') Perennial (Z 6b–10), 4–6' tall, 4' wide, sun to partial shade. A southeastern native, this variegated cultivar is upright with relatively soft, pendent leaf tips. Drought tolerant with 4" white flowers in summer on 3–5' stalks.

'MEDITERRANEAN PINK' HEATHER

(*Erica* × *darleyensis* 'Mediterranean Pink') Perennial (Z 7–8), 1–2' tall, 1–2' wide, sun. Broadleaf evergreen multistem shrub or ground cover. Needlelike leaves in whorls and cylindrical pink flowers on spikes in winter. Prefers acidic soil and good drainage.

'METALLIC BLUE' OUTBACK DAISY

(*Brachyscome* 'Metallic Blue') Annual, 1–2' tall, 2' wide, sun. Hybrid of Australian native with finely divided fernlike foliage and 1"-wide blue daisylike flowers. Requires excellent drainage and is used for rockeries and containers.

MEXICAN FEATHER GRASS

(*Nassella tenuissima*) Perennial (Z 7–10), 1½–2' tall, 1½' wide, sun to partial shade. Clump-forming grass from Texas and Mexico with fine needlelike foliage. In early summer, silky green 1–2" flowers resembling hair mature to golden blond. Tolerates range of soils but not wet feet.

MEXICAN HEATHER

(*Cuphea hyssopifolia*) Annual, 1–3' tall, 3' wide, sun. Well branched subtropical shrub like plant with glossy, linear 1" leaves. Hundreds of small lavender flowers with 6 equal petals appear in leaf axils all summer. Prefers moist well-drained soil.

'MIRACLE WHITE' CYCLAMEN

(*Cyclamen persicum* 'Miracle White') Annual, 5–12" tall, 5–12" wide, shade. Hybrid of Mediterranean native used most often as a houseplant. Prolific upright blooms with swept-back petals and heart-shaped silver marbled leaves. Needs bright indirect light and cool temperatures, 55–70 degrees F.

'MISS HUFF' LANTANA

(*Lantana* 'Miss Huff') Perennial (Z 7b–10), 5–6' tall, 5–6' wide, sun. Tallest and most vigorous lantana. Opposite dentate leaves and orange and pink flowers in clusters from leaf axils. Valued for performance in summer heat. Sterile berries do not reseed. Prefers fertile, well-drained soil.

'MOLINA' IVY GERANIUM

(*Pelargonium* × *peltatum* 'Molina') Annual, 1–3' tall, 3' wide, sun to partial shade. Semidouble, salmon pink flowers on trailing supple stems, with ivy-shaped, leathery leaves and good disease resistance. Performs better with afternoon shade in the South.

'MORNING LIGHT' MISCANTHUS

(*Miscanthus sinensis* 'Morning Light') Perennial (Z 5–9), 4–5' tall, 3' wide, sun to partial shade. Compact ornamental grass with slender leaf blades edged in white giving a luminous effect. Crimson plumes open in late summer and change to tan.

'MRS. MOON' LUNGWORT

(*Pulmonaria saccharata* 'Mrs. Moon') Perennial (Z 3–7), 10–12" tall, 12" wide, partial shade to shade. Clumping woodland plant with silver speckled lance-shaped leaves and pink buds that open blue in early spring. Prefers moist, well-drained soil.

'NEEDLEPOINT' IVY

(*Hedera helix* 'Needlepoint') Perennial (Z 6–10), 10–12" tall, 3–8' wide, sun to shade. Climbing ivy similar to English ivy with palmately lobed shiny dark green leaves but smaller leaf with a long, narrow center lobe. Drought tolerant but prefers rich, moist soils.

'OBOROZUKI' SWEET FLAG ACORUS

(*Acorus gramineus* 'Oborozuki') Perennial (Z 6–10), 8–12" tall, 12" wide, sun to partial shade. Grasslike plant from the Arum family grown for its stiff, evergreen leaf blades with green and gold variegation. Prefers fertile, wet, acidic soil but tolerates normal moist garden soil.

'OGON' SEDUM

(*Sedum makinoi* 'Ogon') Perennial (Z 6–9), 4" tall, 12" wide, sun to partial shade. Prostrate ground-hugging sedum from Japan with golden chartreuse foliage and small yellow flowers in spring. Tolerant of growing conditions but needs well-drained soils. Good in containers and rockeries.

'ORANIA PEACH' SUNSCAPE DAISY

(*Osteospermum ecklonis* 'Orania Peach') Perennial,(Z 9–11), 6–18" tall, 12–18" wide, sun. Hybrid of South African native requiring cool temperature to initiate flowering. Alternate oblong leaves and 2–4" peach daisylike flowers on upright well-branched stems. Best performance in spring.

'ORIENTAL LIMELIGHT' ARTEMISIA

(*Artemisia vulgaris* 'Oriental Limelight') Perennial (Z 3), 12" tall, 24" wide, sun to partial shade. Mounding branching plant grown for light yellow and green variegated, toothed foliage. Spreads by creeping roots.

'ORIGAMI YELLOW' COLUMBINE

(*Aquilegia caerulea* 'Origami Yellow') Perennial (Z 4–7), 16–18" tall, 10–14" wide, sun to partial shade. Graceful plant with spurred pastel yellow flowers and fanlike leaves. This variety blooms from seed first year. Needs moist, well-drained soils and partial shade in hot climates.

PAPERWHITE BULBS

(*Narcissus*) Annual, 10–20" tall, 6–8" wide, sun to partial shade. Nonhardy tazetta daffodils that are produced to be planted and forced into bloom without a cold period. Varieties have white or yellow fragrant flowers and are usually grown indoors in winter.

PARROT'S BEAK

(*Lotus berthelotii*) Annual, 12–18" tall, 18" wide, sun to partial shade. Canary Islands native has mounded growth and scarlet flowers in spring shaped like a beak. Usually grown in containers for its delicate linear silver-cascading foliage. Must have well-drained soil.

'PARTY TIME' JOSEPH'S COAT

(*Alternanthera ficoidea* 'Party Time') Annual, 12" tall, 12" wide, sun to partial shade. Subtropical plant grown for handsome green foliage splashed with pink variegation.

'PEACH SACHET' NEMESIA

(*Nemesia* × *hybrida* 'Peach Sachet') Annual, 1–2' tall, 2' wide, sun to partial shade. Hybrid of South African native has opposite leaves and terminal racemes of 1" peach-colored flowers. These are snapdragonlike and have a light fragrance. Performs best in cool temperatures of spring and fall.

'PEE VEE CEE' ENGLISH IVY
(*Hedera helix* 'Pee Vee Cee') Annual (houseplant), 6–8″ tall, 1–3′ wide, partial shade. Ivy originating in Southern Europe and North America. Trailing habit with dark green, glossy, three-lobed leaves. Prefers indirect or filtered bright light, moderately moist soil, and temperatures between 60 and 85 degrees F.

'PENNY AZURE TWILIGHT' VIOLA
(*Viola cornuta* 'Penny Azure Twilight') Annual, 4–6″ tall, 4–6″ wide, sun to partial shade. Modern hybrid viola with compact, mounding growth habit, and prolific light blue 1–2″ blooms. Performs best in cool temperatures of spring and fall.

'PENNY BLUE' VIOLA
(*Viola cornuta* 'Penny Blue') Annual, 4–6″ tall, 4–6″ wide, sun to partial shade. Modern hybrid viola with compact, mounding growth habit and prolific medium blue 1–2″ blooms. Performs best in cool temperatures of spring and fall.

'PENNY CITRUS MIX' VIOLA
(*Viola cornuta* "Penny Citrus Mix") Annual, 4–6″ tall, 4–6′ wide, sun to partial shade. Modern hybrid viola mix with prolific 1–2″ cream, orange, light and dark yellow blooms and a compact, mounding growth habit. Performs best in cool temperatures of spring and fall.

'PENNY LANE' MIX VIOLA
(*Viola hybrida* 'Penny Lane') Annual, 4– 6″ tall, 4–6″ wide, sun to partial shade. Modern hybrid viola mix with prolific 1–2″ blooms in 14 colors consisting of whites, yellows, and blues. Compact, mounding growth habit; performs best in cool temperatures of spring and fall.

'PENNY VIOLET FLARE' VIOLA
(*Viola cornuta* 'Penny Violet Flare') Annual, 4–6″ tall, 4–6″ wide, sun to partial shade. Modern hybrid viola with compact, mounding growth habit and prolific 1–2″ dark purple blooms with a light center. Performs best in cool temperatures of spring and fall.

'PENNY WHITE' VIOLA
(*Viola cornuta* 'Penny White') Annual, 4–6″ tall, 4–6″ wide, sun to partial shade. Modern hybrid viola with compact, mounding growth habit and prolific white 1–2″ blooms. Performs best in cool temperatures of spring and fall.

PERSIAN SHIELD
(*Strobilanthes dyeranus*) Annual, 3–5′ tall, 3′ wide, sun to partial shade. Upright, soft-stemmed shrub from Myanmar grown for its 6–9″ lanceolate opposite leaves with a purple iridescent sheen rather than its insignificant pale blue flowers. Warm temperatures and sun produce best leaf coloration.

'PICANTE SALMON' SALVIA
(*Salvia splendens* 'Picante Salmon') Annual, 14–16″ tall, 10–12″ wide, sun to partial shade. Vigorous hybrid of Brazilian native with dark green opposite serrated leaves and densely arranged whorls of long-lasting salmon flowers on numerous spikes. Blooms profusely throughout summer and fall.

PLECTRANTHUS
(*Plectranthus fruticosus*) Annual, 18″ tall, 24″ wide, sun to partial shade. South African native grown for its aromatic ornamental foliage rather than its flowers. Dark green leaves with purple undersides on stems that creep and turn upward. Prefers moist, well-drained soil and afternoon shade in hot climates.

'POWIS CASTLE' ARTEMISIA
(*Artemisia* 'Powis Castle') Perennial (Z 6–8), 30″ tall, 3–4′ wide, sun. Shrubby, nonflowering hybrid with finely divided, fernlike, silver foliage forming a mound. Prefers poor, dry soils and will rot in wet conditions.

'PURPLE AND GOLD' LUMINAIRE SERIES TRAILING SNAPDRAGON
(*Antirrhinum majus* 'Purple and Gold') Annual, 12″ tall, 10–12″ wide, sun to partial shade. Frost-tolerant annual with gold and purplish red flowers and trailing habit well suited to containers. Prefers fertile, well-drained soil and feeding at 3-week intervals.

PURPLE CABBAGE
(*Brassica oleracea*) Annual, 10″ tall, 12″ wide, sun. Leafy biennial vegetable often used as ornamental in fall and spring. Grown for colorful leaves, which may or may not form a head, rather than for flowers. If hardened off, it can withstand temperatures of 15 to 20 degrees F.

PURPLE CREEPING THRIFT
(*Phlox subulata*) Perennial (Z 2–9), 4–6″ tall, 2–3′ wide, sun. Spreading evergreen mats of stiff needle-shaped foliage covered with purple flowers in spring. Prefers well-drained, neutral to alkaline soil. Good for rock gardens.

'PURPLE FAN' FANFLOWER
(*Scaevola aemula* 'Purple Fan') Annual, 1′ tall, 18″ wide, sun. Australian native with oblong fleshy 2″ leaves and trailing stems. Solitary purple 1″ fan shaped flowers in leaf axils bloom all summer. Must have well-drained soil.

PURPLE FOUNTAIN GRASS
(*Pennisetum setaceum* 'Rubrum') Annual, 3–4′ tall, 3′ wide, sun. African native grass with thin purple leaves and plumed bristly inflorescence in midsummer that are cream to burgundy. Valuable accent in beds and containers.

PURPLE HEART

(*Tradescantia pallida*) Perennial (Z 7–9), 12–18" tall, 12–14" wide, sun to partial shade. Drought-tolerant Yucatán native grown for vining purple foliage with small pink flowers. Valuable accent in beds and containers. Prefers moist, well-drained soils.

PURPLE KALE

(*Brassica oleracea* 'Acephala') Annual, 8"–3' tall, 7"–2' wide, sun. Leafy biennial vegetable often used as ornamental in fall and spring. Does not form a head. Grown for colorful rosettes of leaves rather than for flowers. If hardened off can withstand temperatures of 15–20 degrees F.

'PURPLE KNIGHT' ALTERNANTHERA

(*Alternanthera dentata* 'Purple Knight') Annual, 16–24" tall, 2–4' wide, sun to partial shade. Purple-foliaged accent plant for beds and containers with vigorous mounding and spreading habit. Pest and disease resistant. Prefers moist, well-drained soils.

'PURPLE LADY' IRESINE

(*Iresine herbstii* 'Purple Lady') Annual, 8" tall, 4' wide, partial sun to shade. Purple foliage accent plant for beds and containers with low-spreading habit. High light and fertility cause crinkled leaf edges.

'PURPLE MAJESTY' ORNAMENTAL MILLET

(*Pennisetum glaucum* 'Purple Majesty') Annual, 4–5' tall, 2–3' wide, sun. Seed-grown ornamental that with sun develops deep purple color from base of stem to tip of its 12–14" flower stalk. Thrives in heat. Disease/pest resistant. All America Selections winner.

'PURPLE MOON" TORENIA

(*Torenia fournieri* hybrid 'Purple Moon') Annual, 6–12" tall, 12–18" wide, sun to partial shade. Vegetative form with square stems, opposite ovate light green leaves and trailing habit. Flowers have 2 lipped corolla with white throats and dark purple outer lobes. Improved sun and heat tolerance. Continuous summer bloom.

'PURPLE ROBE' CUPFLOWER

(*Nierembergia frutescens* "Purple Robe') Annual, 6" tall, 6–12" wide, sun to partial shade. Numerous deep violet-blue cup-shaped flowers produced all spring and summer on slender stems with alternate linear l" leaves.

PURPLE WAFFLE PLANT

(*Pilea cadierii*) Annual, 6–10" tall, 6–12" wide, shade. Vietnamese native grown as houseplant. Metallic purple textured 2–3" leaves grow in opposite pairs on fleshy stems. Prefers indirect light, temperatures between 70 and 85 degrees F., and barely moist soil.

'RACHEL'S GOLD' SALVIA

(*Salvia officinalis* 'Rachel's Gold') Perennial (Z4–7), 12–18" tall, 12–18" wide, sun. Aromatic culinary herb grown for bright chartreuse foliage flecked with darker green accents on leaf margin rather than for flowers. Needs good moisture and drainage.

'RAINBOW' LEUCOTHOE

(*Leucothoe fontanesiana* 'Rainbow') Perennial (shrub), (Z 8), 4' tall, 4' wide, partial shade to shade. Broad-leafed evergreen with arching branches and foliage variegated with cream, yellow, and pink. Weeping clusters of white, urn-shaped flowers in spring. Prefers moist, well-drained soil.

'RAMBLIN' PEACH GLO' PETUNIA

(*Petunia hybrida* 'Ramblin' Peach Glo') Annual, 10–14" tall, 30–36" wide, sun. Vigorous, trailing, early-flowering petunia with 2–3" peach-colored blossoms occurring all over plant including the crown. Useful in beds and containers. Performs best with good moisture and regular fertilization.

'RED BUTTERFLY' PENTAS

(*Pentas lanceolata* "Red Butterfly') Annual, 12–22" tall, 12–20" wide, sun. Vigorous summer bloomer with opposite, lancelet leaves 4–6" long. Star-shaped red flowers with white eyes clustered in 3"-wide wide umbels; tolerant of heat and humidity. Butterfly attractant.

'RED MISSILE' ORNAMENTAL PEPPER

(*Capsicum annuum* 'Red Missile') Annual, 8–10" tall, 8–12" wide, sun. Dwarf compact F-1 hybrid for gardens and containers with clusters of 2" pointed narrow, missilelike fruit that turn from cream to lavender to bright red.

'RED SAIL' LETTUCE

(*Lactuca sativa* 'Red Sail') Annual, 10–12" tall, 10–14" wide, sun. Loose-leaf lettuce with medium green crinkled broad leaves and deeply fringed edges with a burgundy blush. All America Selections winner valued for high vitamin content, mild taste, and resistance to bolting in warm temperatures.

'RED SENSATION' CORDYLINE

(*Cordyline australis* 'Red Sensation') Annual, 4' tall, 3–4' wide, sun to shade. 1 to 2" wide burgundy leaves branch off a fast-growing central stem. Older leaves arch while stiff new growth gives a starburst, structural effect.

RED TWIG DOGWOOD

(*Cornus sericea*) Perennial (shrub) (Z 2–7), 7–9' tall, 10' wide, sun to shade. Broad spreading, multi-stemmed deciduous shrub with stoloniferous habit. Simple ovate opposite leaves 2–5" long and attractive red stems in fall and winter. Not tolerant of heat and humidity.

'REFLECTIONS LAVENDER' PETUNIA
Annual, 8–14″ tall, 12–24″ wide, sun to partial shade. Vigorous trailing, early-flowering petunia with alternate leaves and numerous frilly double lavender flowers that cover entire plant and are produced all summer.

'ROCKY MOUNTAIN LIGHT PINK' GERANIUM
(*Pelargonium* × *hortorum* 'Rocky Mountain Light Pink') Annual, 14–16″ tall, 12–18″ wide, sun to partial shade. Semidouble light pink flowers in umbels held above foliage bloom all summer. Orbicular-shaped leaves. Vigorous plant with excellent heat tolerance.

'ROCKY MOUNTAIN SALMON' GERANIUM
(*Pelargonium* × *hortorum* 'Rocky Mountain Salmon') Annual, 14–16″ tall, 12–18″ wide, sun to partial shade. Semidouble salmon flowers in umbels held above foliage bloom all summer. Orbicular-shaped leaves with dark horseshoe-shaped zone on each leaf. Vigorous plant with excellent heat tolerance.

'ROYAL CANDLES' VERONICA
(*Veronica spicata* 'Royal Candles') Perennial (Z 3–7), 15–18″ tall, 12–18″ wide, sun to partial shade, Rigidly upright, compact growth with sturdy spikes of blue flowers in late spring, early summer. Bottom foliage stays attractive more than most varieties.

'ROYAL HERITAGE' STRAIN HELLEBORE
(*Helleborus* 'Royal Heritage') Perennial (Z 4–9), 18–24″ tall, 12–18″ wide, partial shade. Low-maintenance, clump-forming evergreen with compound palmate leaves and 2–3″ flowers in wide range of colors that bloom in late winter and last for weeks. Best in partial shade, well-drained soil.

'RUBY STAR' CONEFLOWER
(*Echinacea purpurea* 'Ruby Star') Perennial (Z 3–9), 36–40″ tall, 18″ wide, sun. Upright clump-forming U.S. prairie native with lance-shaped leaves and dark pink flowers with orange central cones. This seed-grown selection has larger rosier flowers than species.

'SALEM' ROSEMARY
(*Rosmarinus officinalis* 'Salem') Perennial (Z 6), 12–18″ tall, 12–18″ wide, sun. Mediterranean evergreen shrub with aromatic needlelike leaves, woody stems, blue flowers. Valued culinary herb. This North Carolina selection has a tidy upright habit. Needs well-drained soil.

'SALSA LIGHT PURPLE' SALVIA
(*Salvia splendens* 'Salsa Light Purple') Annual, 12–14″ tall, 10–12″ wide, sun to partial shade. Compact hybrid of Brazilian native with dark green opposite serrated leaves and densely arranged whorls of light purple flowers on numerous spikes. Blooms profusely throughout summer and fall.

'SALSA PURPLE' SALVIA
(*Salvia splendens* 'Salsa Purple') Annual, 12–14″ tall, 10–12″ wide, sun to partial shade. Compact hybrid of Brazilian native with dark green opposite serrated leaves and densely arranged whorls of dark purple flowers on numerous spikes. Blooms profusely throughout summer and fall.

'SALSA ROSE' SALVIA
(*Salvia splendens* 'Salsa Rose') Annual, 12–14″ tall, 10–12″ wide, sun to partial shade. Compact hybrid of Brazilian native with dark green opposite serrated leaves and densely arranged whorls of dusty warm pink flowers on numerous spikes. Blooms profusely throughout summer and fall.

'SAN TAKAO' AUTUMN SAGE
(*Salvia greggii* 'San Takao') Perennial (Z 8–10), 2–3′ tall, 3′ wide, sun. Hybrid of Mexican native with shrubby growth habit and tolerance for heat, humidity, and drought. Has 1–2″-long ovate entire leaves and 2-lipped mauve pink flowers in whorls of 2 or 3 that bloom from midsummer through fall.

'SARATOGA LIME' NICOTIANA
(*Nicotiana alata* 'Saratoga Lime') Annual, 10–12″ tall, 10–12″ wide, sun to shade. Compact hybrid nicotiana with bushy habit, large wavy alternate leaves, and trumpet-shaped fragrant lime green flowers on terminal panicles. Plants are at their best on cooler days of spring and fall.

'SASSY' BOSTON FERN
(*Nephrolepis exalta* 'Sassy') Annual (houseplant), 8–10″ tall, 14″ wide, bright indirect light. Compact Boston fern used as table fern or in small basket. Light green uniform fronds with a spreading, globose habit. Prefers temperatures between 60 and 75 degrees.

'SCHOENE HELENA' GERANIUM
(*Pelargonium* × *hortorum* 'Schoene Helena') Annual, 14–16″ tall, 12–18″ wide, sun to partial shade. Semidouble salmon flowers in umbels held above foliage bloom all summer. Orbicular-shaped green leaves. Vigorous plant with good heat tolerance.

SEA-PINKS
(*Armeria maritima* 'Splendens') Perennial (Z 4–8), 6–8″ tall, 6–10″ wide, sun to partial shade. Low-growing evergreen perennial with grassy foliage in rounded clumps. Rosy pink ball-shaped flowers in spring and early summer. Used in rock garden or as edging. Prefers light soils.

'SEASIDE' SUNSCAPE DAISY
(*Osteospermum fruticosum* 'Seaside') Perennial (Z 9–11), 6–18″ tall, 18–24″ wide, sun. Hybrid of South African native requiring cool temperature to initiate flowering. Alternate oblong leaves and 2–4″ pink and white daisylike flowers on upright well-branched stems. Best performance in spring.

'SENTIMENTAL BLUE' BALLOON FLOWER
(*Platycodon grandiflorus* 'Sentimental Blue') Perennial (Z 4–9), 6–8″ tall, 8–12″ wide, sun to partial shade. Late-emerging perennial has compact growth habit, opposite, toothed, triangular leaves, and large blue balloon-shaped buds that open to 5-petaled, star-shaped flowers with dark blue veins. Blooms several weeks in summer.

SHRIMP PLANT
(*Pachystachys lutea*) Annual, 3′ tall, 3′ wide, sun to partial shade. Tropical plant with dark green leaves and scores of bright yellow 5–6″ upright bracts that support tiny white flowers for summer-long color. Appreciates moist, well-drained soil and filtered afternoon light.

'SILHOUETTE APPLEBLOSSOM' DOUBLE IMPATIENS
(*Impatiens walleriana* 'Silhouette Appleblossom') Annual, 12″ high, 8–12″ wide, shade to partial shade. Double flowers in soft pink bloom from May to frost.

SILVER CUBAN OREGANO
(*Plectranthus argentatus*) Annual, 2–3′ tall, 3′ wide, sun. Vigorous Australian native grown as foliage accent. Branching erect subshrub with downy silver 4″ ovate opposite leaves. Insignificant light blue flowers. Performs well in hot conditions.

'SILVER DRAGON' LILYTURF
(*Liriope spicata* 'Silver Dragon') Perennial (Z 6–9), 8″ tall, 8–10″ wide, sun to shade. Evergreen ground cover with narrow, silvery white striped leaves and pale purple flowers in late summer.

'SILVER MIST' LICORICE PLANT
(*Helichrysum petiolatum* 'Silver Mist') Annual, 6–8″ tall, 12–18″ wide, sun. Accent plant for containers and beds with spreading mounds of silver foliage and stems. Tiny, round, finely textured leaves thrive in fertile, well-drained, somewhat dry soil. Tolerates heat.

'SILVER MOUND' ARTEMISIA
(*Artemisia schmidtiana* 'Silver Mound') Perennial (Z 3–7), 3–10″ tall, 24–30″ wide, sun to partial shade. Compact mounded foliage plant with fernlike silver leaves. Used for rock gardens and edgings. Needs well-drained soil.

SILVER SEDGE
(*Carex platyphylla*) Perennial (Z 3–8), 6–12″ tall, 12″ wide, partial shade to shade. Shade-loving ground cover with 1″-wide silver-green leaves.

'SILVER SPIKE' HELICHRYSUM
(*Helichrysum thianschaicum* 'Silver Spike') Annual, 6–12″ high, 18–24″ wide, partial shade. Foliage is brightly silvered and has a mild curry fragrance. Its naturally spiky form adds texture to plantings. Drought tolerant.

'SNOWCAP' HOSTA
(*Hosta* 'Snowcap') Perennial (Z 3–9), 30″ tall, 40″ wide, partial to full shade. Handsome ground cover for shade with durable blue-green leaves accented with cream-white margin and white flowers in midsummer. Protect from dry soil, afternoon sun, slugs, and deer.

SOCIETY GARLIC
(*Tulbaghia violacea*) Perennial (Z 7–10), 18–30″ tall, 18″ wide, sun to partial shade. Vigorous, clump-forming tender perennial with narrow, gray-green aromatic leaves and umbels of lilac flowers held on tall stalks. Blooms sporadically from spring to fall.

'SONIC LIGHT PINK' NEW GUINEA IMPATIENS
(*Impatiens* × hybrida 'Sonic Light Pink') Annual, 10–12″ tall, 10–12″ wide, shade to partial sun. Extra-large, soft pink, flat-faced, long-spurred blooms that can take full sun if plant is kept consistently moist. Colors stay bright in shade. Dark green lance-shaped foliage with fleshing stems. Blooms from May to frost.

'SONIC WHITE' NEW GUINEA IMPATIENS
(*Impatiens* × hybrida 'Sonic White') Annual, 10–12″ tall, 10–12″ wide, shade to partial sun. Pure white large-petaled, long-spurred blooms that grow in sun with plenty of moisture. Colors stay bright in shade. Dark lance-shaped green foliage with fleshy stems. Blooms from May to frost.

'SORBET BLUE HEAVEN' VIOLA
(*Viola cornuta* 'Sorbet Blue Heaven') Annual, 6–8″ tall, 6–8″ wide, sun to partial shade. Modern hybrid viola with compact growth habit and free-flowering violet blue 1–2″ blooms. Performs best in cool temperature of spring and fall.

'SOUTHERN CHARM' ORNAMENTAL MULLEIN
(*Verbascum* × hybrida 'Southern Charm') Perennial (Z 5–9), 24–36″ tall, 18″ wide, sun. Clump-forming rosette of leaves and long-blooming spikes of 1″ flowers in pink, apricot, and cream shades. Prefers well-drained soil.

'SPARKLING BURGUNDY' PINEAPPLE LILY
(*Eucomis comosa* 'Sparkling Burgundy') Perennial
(Z 6b–9), 24″ tall, 24″ tall, sun to partial shade. Clumping
deciduous plant produces rosette of dark burgundy straplike
leaves and in summer 20″ bloom stalk resembling purple
pineapple. Drought tolerant.

**STAINED GLASSWORKS 'FRIGHT NIGHT'
COLEUS**
(*Solenostemon scutellariodes* 'Fright Night') Annual, 20–36″
tall, 12–30″ wide, sun to partial shade. Vigorous upright hybrid of Asian native grown for colorful foliage. Strong square
branching stems of long narrow crotonlike leaves of yellow
and pink fringed in olive. Prefers rich, well-drained soil.

STAINED GLASSWORKS 'KIWI FERN' COLEUS
(*Solenostemon scutellariodes* 'Kiwi Fern') Annual, 8–18″ tall,
9–15″ wide, sun to partial shade. Vigorous hybrid of Asian
native used for colorful foliage. Has opposite elongated
leaves with maroon centers and deeply fingered, golden leaf
margins densely packed on square stems. Prefers rich, well-
drained soil.

**STAINED GLASSWORKS 'SWISS SUNSHINE'
COLEUS**
(*Solenostemon scutellariodes* 'Swiss Sunshine') Annual,
20–24″ tall, 9–15″ wide, sun to partial shade. Vigorous
trailing hybrid of Asian native used for colorful foliage.
Square stems and relatively small opposite leaves with pink
centers and light green toothed edges. Prefers rich, well-
drained soils.

STAINED GLASSWORKS 'TILT A WHIRL' COLEUS
(*Solenostemon scutellariodes* 'Tilt a Whirl') Annual, 20–24″
tall, 9–15″ wide, sun to partial shade. Vigorous upright hybrid of Asian native used for foliage. Square stems and
unique rounded leaves have yellow to apple green centers,
sharply toothed yellow margins, and a red interior. Prefers
rich, well-drained soils.

**STAINED GLASSWORKS 'TRAILING ROSE'
COLEUS**
(*Solenostemon scutellariodes* 'Trailing Rose') Annual, 8–12″
tall, 1½–3′ wide, sun to partial shade. Vigorous trailing hybrid of Asian native used for colorful foliage. Square stems
and opposite burgundy leaves have fuchsia pink center and
chartreuse edge. Prefers rich, well-drained soil.

**'STEPHANIE' PROPHET SERIES
CHRYSANTHEMUM**
(*Chrysanthemum* × *morifolium* 'Stephanie') Perennial
(Z 4–9), 1–2′ high, 18–26″ wide, sun. Snow-white daisy
flowers with prolific display in mid-September. Large
cushion to ball-shaped plant.

STRAWBERRY BEGONIA
(*Saxifraga stolonifera*) Perennial (Z 5–10), 6–8″ tall, 12″
wide, sun to partial shade. Asian native with rounded glossy
leaves that are olive green with silver veins and pink undersides. Oddly petaled white flowers bloom on thin erect
stalks in spring/summer. Spreads by runners.

STRAWBERRY FOXGLOVE
(*Digitalis* × *mertonensis*) Perennial (Z 3–8), 2–3′ tall, 12″
wide, partial shade. Hybrid foxglove forms rosette of large,
dark green leathery leaves and tall spikes of rose-pink
spotted flowers that appear on one side of stem. Short lived,
to 2–3 years. Needs moist soils.

'SUM AND SUBSTANCE' HOSTA
(*Hosta* 'Sum and Substance') Perennial (Z 3–9), 36″ tall, 60″
wide, sun to shade. Handsome ground cover for shade with
huge, rounded, chartreuse-green leaves of thick substance.
Light lavender flowers on 60″ scapes. Needs some sun for
best leaf coloration.

**'SUNNY LINDA' PROPHET SERIES
CHRYSANTHEMUM**
(*Chrysanthemum* × *morifolium* 'Sunny Linda') Perennial
(Z 4–9), 1–2′ high, 18–26″ wide, sun. Fresh, light yellow
flowers averaging 2″ in diameter and made up of ray petals.
Compact, spreading habit. Blooms in late September.

'SUPER PARFAIT RASPBERRY' DIANTHUS
(*Dianthus chinensis* 'Super Parfait Raspberry') Annual, 6–8″
tall, 8–10″ wide, full sun. Deep pink and white petals with a
burgundy eye. Prefers well-drained soil.

'SWEET AUTUMN' CLEMATIS
(*Clematis paniculata* 'Sweet Autumn') Perennial (Z 5–9),
10–20′ tall, sun to partial shade. Climbing vine with lus-
trous, leathery dark green leaves. Masses of fragrant creamy
white ½–1″ flowers in late summer and fall. Prune severely to
control height.

'SWEET KATE' SPIDERWORT
(*Tradescantia* × *andersoniana* 'Sweet Kate') Perennial
(Z 3–9), 12″ tall, 10–18″ wide, partial shade. Chartreuse grasslike foliage contrasts in late spring/early summer with numerous 3-petaled deep blue flowers with yellow anthers, each
bloom lasting only a day. Prefers moist, well-drained soil.

'TEMPLEHOF' HINOKI FALSE CYPRESS
(*Chamaecyparis obtusa* 'Templehof') Perennial shrub,
(Z 5–8), 5′ tall, 3′ wide, sun to partial shade. Vigorous,
low-growing evergreen shrub with dense, conical form.
Flattened sprays of green to yellow-green foliage on
fan-shaped branches. Valuable accent plant.

'TOFFEE TWIST' SEDGE

(*Carex flagellifera* 'Toffee Twist') Perennial (Z 7–9), 2–3' tall, 2–3' wide, sun to partial shade. New Zealand evergreen species forms spreading clump of fine, curled tufts of coppery bronze foliage which takes on coral tones in fall/winter. Good in containers and rockeries.

'TOJEN' TOAD LILY

(*Tricyrtis hirta* 'Tojen') Perennial (Z 4–8), 18–24" tall, 10–14" wide, partial shade to shade. Clump-forming plants with graceful arching ladderlike leaves that alternate up the stems. Orchidlike lavender flowers with white centers appear in late summer. Moist soils prevent leaf scorch.

'TOLIMA' CHRYSANTHEMUM

(*Chrysanthemum* × *morifolium* 'Tolima') Perennial (Z 4–9), 1–2' high, 18–26" wide, sun. White to light yellow blooms that flower in mid-September. A spray mum flower form more than 1½" in diameter, comprised almost entirely of ray petals. It is usually flat or slightly crested in appearance.

'TOP HIT' PINK HYACINTHS

(*Hyacinthus orientalis* 'Top Hit') Perennial (Z 4–8), 8–10" tall, 6" wide, sun to partial shade. Upright pest-resistant plant from bulb blooms in early spring with fragrant, soft lilac tubular florets covering rigid 10" stem. Valuable for flowerbeds and indoor forcing.

'TRICOLOR' SAGE

(*Salvia officinalis* 'Tricolor') Perennial (Z 5–8), 12–18" tall, 18" wide, sun to partial shade. Ornamental selection of culinary herb with variegated leaves of gray-green, cream, and pink on burgundy stems. Compact growth habit and flavorful leaves. Prefers well-drained soil.

TRIUMPH TYPE, SOFT PINK TULIP

Perennial bulb (Z 3–7), 16–22" tall, 6" wide, sun to partial shade. Triumph variety tulips have sturdy stems and "traditional" tulip-shaped blooms in many colors. They bloom in early to mid spring.

TROPICAL BUTTERFLY WEED

(*Asclepias curassavica*) Annual, 28–40" tall, 12–18" wide, sun. Upright tropical native with long, narrow leaves and flat umbels of numerous red and orange flowers. Used in beds as ornamentals, butterfly attractants, and cut flowers. Flowers the first year from seed. Sap can be a skin and eye irritant.

'VALERIE FINNIS' MUSCARI

(*Muscari armeniacum* 'Valerie Finnis') Perennial (Z 4–9), 6–8" tall, 6" wide, sun to partial shade. Small, pest-resistant plant from bulb sends up slender grasslike foliage in fall and spikes of pale lavender grapelike flowers in early spring.

'VALLEY ROSE' JAPANESE ANDROMEDA

(*Pieris japonica* 'Valley Rose') Perennial (shrub), (Z 5–8), 10–12' tall, 6–8' wide, sun to partial shade. Broad-leaved evergreen with oblong glossy leathery leaves and pale waxy pink flowers in pendulous terminal clusters. Prefers moist, acidic, well-drained soil.

'VANILLA SACHET' NEMESIA

(*Nemesia* × *hybrida* 'Vanilla Sachet') Annual, 10" tall, 9" wide, sun to partial shade. Cultivar of South African native with 1–3" long spatulalike leaves and ½–1" wide white fragrant flowers with yellow throats that bloom in terminal clusters. Best in cool temperatures of spring and fall.

VARIEGATED 'CHARMS PINK' BEGONIA

(*Begonia semperflorens* 'Charms Pink') Annual, 15" tall, 18" wide, partial shade. Double pink flowers with bright green and cream marbled foliage. Upright growth habit. Performs best with regular fertilization and soil allowed to dry slightly between waterings.

VARIEGATED CUBAN OREGANO

(*Plectranthus amboinicus*) Annual, 1–2' tall, 3' wide, sun to partial shade. South African native with thick, green and white 4" leaves on trailing stems that turn up at the ends. Pungent foliage. Withstands heat and humidity.

VARIEGATED FLAX LILY

(*Dianella tasmanica* 'Variegata') Perennial (Z 8–10), 4' tall, 3' wide, partial shade to full shade. Species from Australia and Tasmania that spreads from rhizomes and has arching straplike green and white leaves. Star-shaped blue flowers on 3' stems in spring followed by blue berries in fall.

'VARIEGATED MINT ROSE' SCENTED GERANIUM

(*Pelargonium graveolens* 'Variegated Mint Rose') Annual, 1–2' tall, 1–2' wide, sun to partial shade. South African native with deeply lobed furry variegated pale green leaves that give aroma of roses and mint when brushed. Small 5-petaled pink flowers. Prefers well-drained soil.

VARIEGATED PORCELAIN VINE

(*Ampelopsis brevipedunculata* 'Elegans') Perennial (Z 4–8), 10–25' tall, 12–15' wide, sun to partial shade. Vigorous vine with large grape-leaf-shaped green and white speckled foliage. Creamy white flowers and in fall ½" berries. Best variegation in partial shade but best fruiting in sun.

'VARIEGATUS' JAPANESE SILVER GRASS

(*Miscanthus sinensis* 'Variegatus') Perennial (Z 6–9), 4–6' tall, 4–5' wide, sun to partial shade. Medium-textured foliage with green and white stripes and a graceful arching habit. Reddish flower plumes in early fall.

'VELOUR BLUE BRONZE' VIOLA
(*Viola* × *wittrockiana* 'Velour Blue Bronze') Annual, 6–8″ tall, 6–8″ wide, sun to partial shade. Numerous 1″ flowers with a blue "cap" and red bronze "face" and a dark center. Cool-season annual usually planted in fall or spring. Frequent fertilization improves bloom.

VELVET DUSTY MILLER
(*Centaurea gymnocarpa*) Perennial (Z 8–10), 2–3′ tall, 1½–2′ wide, sun to partial shade. Silvery gray foliage plant with 8″ felty, pinnately dissected leaves that grow from a central stem. Used as accent plants in beds and containers.

VERBENA-ON-A-STICK
(*Verbena bonariensis*) Perennial (Z 7–10), 3– 5′ tall, 2–3′ wide, sun to partial shade. Airy South American native with upright growth habit and numerous branching, square stems topped with 2″ clusters of tiny lavender flowers. Blooms spring through fall.

'VICTORIA BLUE' SALVIA
(*Salvia farinacea* 'Victoria Blue') Perennial (Z 8–10), 18–36″ tall, 1–2″ wide, sun to partial shade. Fast-growing Texas native with narrow, oval 3″ leaves and numerous terminal spikes densely covered with ¼″-long tubular violet-blue flowers that bloom all spring and summer.

'WEEPING LAVENDER' LANTANA
(*Lantana montevidensis* 'Weeping Lavender') Tender perennial or annual (Z 8 – 11), 6–12″ tall, 24–36″ wide, sun to partial shade. Beautiful trailing or spreading habit with profusion of lavender flowers which attract butterflies. Heat, wind, and drought tolerant.

WHISPERS 'APPLEBLOSSOM' PETUNIA
(*Petunia hybrida* 'Appleblossom') Annual, 6–10″ tall, 18–24″ wide, sun to partial shade. Vigorous hybrid mini-petunia with numerous pale pink funnel-shaped flowers on a spreading plant with alternate entire leaves. Flowers cover entire plant and are produced all summer.

WHISPERS 'BLUE ROSE' PETUNIA
(*Petunia hybrida* 'Blue Rose') Annual, 6–10″ tall, 18–24″ wide, sun to partial shade. Vigorous hybrid mini-petunia with numerous blue rose funnel-shaped flowers on a spreading plant with alternate entire leaves. Flowers cover entire plant and are produced all summer

WHITE BUTTON-TYPE CHRYSANTHEMUM
(*Chrysanthemum* × *morifolium*) Perennial (Z 4–9), 18″–2′ high, 18–20″ wide, sun. Pure white button-shaped blooms that flower in mid-September.

'WHITE CRANE' FLOWERING KALE
(*Brassica oleracea* 'White Crane') Annual, 12–24″ tall, 6–8″ wide, sun. F-1 hybrid ornamental kale is creamy ivory with dark green outer leaves and a pink center. Small head on sturdy stems makes it useful in beds and containers and as long-lasting cut flower. Prefers cool temperatures.

WHITE MOTH ORCHID
(*Phalaenopsis* hybrids) Annual, 18–24″ tall, 8–12″ wide, filtered light. Tropical or subtropical plants with broad leaves that spring directly from roots and tall arching stems with large rounded white flowers resembling moths. Needs filtered light, constant moisture, and perfect drainage.

'WHITE SACHET' NEMESIA
(*Nemesia* × *hybrida* 'White Sachet') Annual, 10″ tall, 9″ wide, sun to partial shade. Cultivar of South African native with 1–3″-long spatulalike leaves and ½–1″-wide white fragrant flowers with yellow throats that bloom in terminal clusters. Best in cool temperatures of spring and fall.

'WILDSIDE' SUNSCAPE DAISY
(*Osteospermum fruticosum* 'Wildside') Perennial (Z 9–11), 6–18″ tall, 18–24″ wide, sun. Hybrid of South African native requiring cool temperature to initiate flowering. Alternate oblong leaves and 2–4″-purple daisylike flowers on upright well-branched stems. Best performance in spring.

YELLOW BELLS
(*Tecoma stans*) Annual, 6–15′ tall, 1–4′ wide, sun. Shrublike tropical with glossy compound leaves of 5–7 serrated leaflets and 2″ bright yellow trumpet-shaped flowers at branch tips attractive to butterflies and hummingbirds. Prefers moist soils.

YELLOW GERBERA DAISIES
(*Gerbera jamesonii*) Annual, 1–3′ tall, 12–18″ wide, sun to partial shade. South African native forms basal rosette of deeply lobed, lance-shaped leaves and 3″-wide daisylike flower heads born singly on long stems in spring and summer. Popular cut and garden flower.

'YELLOW NICOLE' CHRYSANTHEMUM
(*Chrysanthemum* × *morifolium* 'Yellow Nicole') Perennial (Z 4–9), 1–2′ tall, 1–2′ wide, full sun to partial shade. Early flowering, light yellow decorative bloom. Flowers around August 30.

'YUBI SUMMER JOY' ORANGE MOSS ROSE
(*Portulaca grandiflora* 'Yubi Summer Joy') Annual, 2–4″ tall, 8–12″ wide, sun. Indian native with flat, ovate succulent leaves on a prostrate, trailing plant. Single vivid orange 2–2 3/4″ flowers bloom from spring to frost and close in cloudy conditions. Prefers well-drained soil and hot, dry conditions.

Acknowledgments

Such a book could never be assembled without the help of so many talented and dedicated people. The idea of a container book based upon a cookbook model packed full of delicious recipes required an army of chefs, numerous test kitchens, and lots of discriminating "tasters" to sample the final confections.

This endeavor required the full support and enthusiasm of my publisher, Clarkson Potter, for which I am most grateful. I thank the entire staff for their commitment to crafting exceptional books. Lauren Shakely for her unyielding support and vision, Natalie Kaire for her guidance through the manuscript, and Marysarah Quinn for outstanding creative design sensibilities. Thanks also to Jane Treuhaft, Mark McCauslin, and Joan Denman for shepherding the book through production.

I am particularly grateful to Betsy Lyman for her boundless enthusiasm for this project since its inception. Her thoughtful insight, steadfast dedication, and resourceful solutions led us to a book that is both beautiful and useful.

I am indebted to Betty Freeze, who worked tirelessly with me to bring together winning combinations, all the while helping me assess and record our victories and failures.

I thank both Jane Colclasure and Kelly Quinn for their masterful photography. Together they captured the heart of each container's design and the essence of the ideas behind the entire book.

Many thanks also to Mary Ellen Pyle for sorting through the endless details of compiling the plant names and descriptions for the recipes and to Nicole Claas for organizing the photo library.

I am also grateful to our entire production and design team who all played important roles in the development of the book and who continue to communicate the ideas and principles behind it, including Mindy Hawes, Josh Hubbard, Ward Lile, Pam Holden, Christy McWilliams, Jefferson Davis, Mandy Shoptaw, Todd Orr, David Curran, Yutaro Kobayashi, Bill Reishtein, Doug Buford, and Kathlyn Graves.

Throughout this project so many generously shared their beautiful gardens, containers, and plants to ensure the book's success. I thank Reed and Rebecca Thompson, Ronnie and Patty Pyle, Robert and Mary Lynn Dudley, Mark and Cheri Nichols, Robert and Gaye Anderson, Overton and Kay Anderson, Paul and Bonnie Wallace, Carl Miller, Scott and Sharon Mosely, Mark and Kim Brockinton, Joe and Judith Colclasure, Claiborne and Elaine Deming, Jim Dyke and Helen Porter, Sally Foley, Henry and Marilyn Lile, Cathy Hamilton Mayton and Mike Mayton of Hamilton Mayton English Antiques, Duncan and Nancy Porter, Rick Smith and Susan Sims Smith, Bill and Kathy Worthen, Brian Hardin, Norma Ryall, Warren and Harriet Stephens, Janet Fox, Vicky Holt, and Mike and Kelly Freeze.

Thanks to Josh Hubbard, Chris Smith, and Matt Parker, who did the backbreaking work of caring for and often moving these containers from one location to another. Equally I thank Ken Hughes and Dwight Westerman for their craftsmanship and help along the way.

Throughout the development of the container recipes we had tremendous support and exceptional plant materials from The Flower Fields, Donna Greenbush, Faith Savage, Ron Garofalo; Carolina Nursery, J. and Linda Guy; Imperial Nursery, Greg Schaan; Willoway Nursery, Tom Demoline; Conrad-Pyle Nursery, Steve Hutton; and Beds & Borders, Inc., Kathryn Pufahl.

And from the following garden centers: Cantrell Gardens, Lakewood Gardens, Maumelle Nursery, Hocott's Garden Center, The Good Earth Garden Center, Brent & Becky's Bulbs, Sally Ferguson and the Netherlands Flower Bulb Information Center, and City Farmer.

And certainly this book would be pointless without vessels for various recipes to call home. I appreciate all the support from the following companies for providing so many quality products: Norcal Pottery Products, New England Pottery, Green Piece Wire Art, Achla Design—Indro Trade Corp., Tuscan Imports, Fiskars, Earthbox, Dripworks, Caffco, Normandy Imports, Meyer Imports, Braun Horticulture, and Flower Framers by Jay.

Index